LOVE IN A DAMP CLIMATE

To all those who shared their stories

First published in 2008 by
CURRACH PRESS
55A Spruce Avenue, Stillorgan Industrial Park, Blackrock, Co. Dublin
www.currach.ie
1 3 5 4 2
Cover design by design-bos.ie
Origination by Currach Press
Printed in Ireland by ColourBooks, Baldoyle Industrial Estate, Dublin 13
ISBN: 978-1-85607-974-7

LOVE IN A DAMP CLIMATE

THE DATING GAME…IRISH STYLE

QUENTIN FOTTRELL

CURRACH PRESS

ACKNOWLEDGEMENTS

Thank you to every person who wrote into WorldWeary.com over the years asking for advice on break-ups, break-downs, relationships and sexcapades, and to those who agreed to be interviewed for this book. Thanks too to Ray D'Arcy, Jenny Kelly, Will Hanafin, Mairéad Farrell, Siobhán Hogan and Martin Maguire for their good humour and loyalty. A big thank you to Aisli Madden from www.designbos.ie, who created the perfect cover design. Thanks to my publisher Jo O'Donoghue at Currach Press and publicist Gráinne Ross for their patience and hard work. To my family, friends and, last but not least, Himself – the title of this book begins and ends with you.

CONTENTS

PREFACE

'You broke my heart,' I said.

It was not the most original line and it makes me cringe to think of it even now but it felt good to get that off my chest. It seemed like a good opening gambit for the end of the affair. I wanted my ex to feel guilty, to see the collateral damage that was done to that most delicate of organs.

'You broke your own heart,' came the unexpected reply.

That kind of language on this, our last date, wasn't exactly what I'd signed up for on our first. It was over now and I was feeling self-righteous grief and, frankly, disbelief. How could I not be loved back? Me, the protagonist in my own love story? It had taken a long time to make my choice. What a cheek.

I now understood every cheap song lyric. Every time I turned on the radio, my kitchen-sink drama replayed all over again.

On a happier note, the real drama started here.

In time, I thought about it some more. It wasn't such a bad experience. I had learnt a lot about the high expectations we put on others and ourselves, which few of us can live up to. And just because the relationship ended didn't necessarily mean it wasn't a success. We could be friends. In time.

I wasn't always so logical. In the immediate aftermath of the break-up, I went a bit loopy. 'Why?' I asked whoever would listen.

After a while, I realised that I was rather enjoying this. It was even more fun than the relationship! I was still the protagonist in my own love story and now the stage was all mine. No nasty exes to mess up my drama. For a while, misery was a lot of fun.

How to mend a broken heart is not the kind of thing they teach you in home economics class. It's something we have to learn for ourselves, with our takeaway dinners and those song lyrics.

Like 'L is For Lover' by Al Jarreau: 'Do not cry for the love you lost,' he sang. And, 'Do not cry for the love you need.'

You know, he had a point. There are many false remedies.

Revenge sex: 'Who would my ex-lover most hate me to sleep with? The best friend? Or worst enemy?' Some do it.

Ex-sex: 'That's your lot. Loser!'

Crazy sex. 'We're doing that now? What if we lose the key?'

Good sex. Bad sex. No sex. Meaningful sex: 'Must I put my heart back on the line? It's been through so much already.'

How would I know when the right person came along again? What if the right person became the wrong person? Or if the right person merely did a wrong thing? How do I make myself available again? Do I change my behaviour? Go to a different bar? Set up an online profile? Join a running club? Take up bridge? Do like the Americans and always be open to meeting someone, whether I'm in a bookshop, sitting on the Luas or feeding the ducks in the park?

I didn't know the answers to those questions. Yet.

Reading is the best way of travelling without going anywhere. A friend once told me that P.G. Wodehouse saved her life. What was that strange stirring in the pit of my stomach? Was it the shellfish I had for lunch? No. Goodbye, self-pity. Hello, empathy. One of the many benefits of reading and getting lost in a good book.

I stopped thinking about my relationship, about myself. I went to museums and gazed at portraits of people who had lived a hundred years ago. They were dead now. I wasn't. That put my broken heart in perspective. I stopped drowning my sorrows and started eating healthier food. I even tried cooking. I joined a gym.

Did millions of people around the world really go through this too? It took only a few moments to fall head-first down the rabbit hole but it would take a hell of a long time to crawl my way back. I suddenly had so much more respect for the human race. 'You give me good advice,' a friend told me, 'so why don't you take your own advice?'

So I added something else to my list. I dusted myself off. I would give the advice instead. I set up my own website, WorldWeary.com, as an agony uncle. I started with the point of view of a peer, not a therapist. That was seven years ago and the letters keep coming.

I wanted to put all this into a book, not just give advice. So, for this book, I spent my spare time travelling around Ireland listening instead of giving advice, collecting stories from people, young and old: dates that went horribly wrong; relationships that worked out and those that didn't; friendships that endured outside of romantic love; and other friendationships that over time turned into something else entirely.

It's not about money. Despite what we had been led to believe these last ten years, I don't believe we are these money-hungry, beer-swilling so-and-sos. These relationships, past and present, romantic or platonic, define us. They say a lot about who we are and how far we have come. I like us. We're not so bad, after all.

I felt better already.

1

You've Got Male

Imagination is the precious commodity dating websites supply. It is what keeps people clicking. It's the eternal promise of fulfilling your wildest sexual fantasies or most romantic dreams, or both. He or she is just around the next virtual corner.

It's the real-life weird science, where lonely hearts type their requirements for the kind of person they would like to meet: height, gender, hair colour, body type, sexual preferences, whether they're looking for sex, a relationship, friendship or all three, then press return and…

You can talk to them online one minute and they can be sitting in your living room, flesh and blood, the next. There could be a matinee idol in there. Or he could suffer from blowfish syndrome: all puffed up with self-confidence online but a salivating, nervous geek a few inches shorter than you expected when he turns up on your doorstep.

Throw him back to the blowfish bowl.

Be warned. You may discover that ShiningKnight45 was that guy you flirted with when you were drunk, when you were lonely, who was SexManiac48. PrincessBride38 could be BitchSlap33, the same darling girl you spoke to two months ago, only now she's got a more sexual profile and is five years younger.

People cruise and socialise online, as they have always cruised in bars, beaches and on the 46A bus. It's just faster and more efficient. On Facebook, you can send a virtual vampire after someone, you can super-poke someone by giving them virtual flowers, a virtual hug or a pinch or, if you like, you can 'select all' and hug all your friends at once.

US-based Match.com and Nerve.com, which is sexier, have helped to take the shame out of online dating.

Americans market themselves far more successfully. Arguably, they are a more attractive and athletic bunch, genetically modified by years of immigration and cross-cultural pollination. They also understand lighting and the importance of good spelling and good teeth.

The Internet is many things. It is nothing if not an endless pool of possibilities which can be highly addictive, a tantalising bottle of whiskey that never runs out.

On Gaydar.ie, the popular gay website, one guy met a bloke who turned out to be his second cousin. 'I love hairy chests and I love Guinness so I poured Guinness over his chest and…' There's an advertising slogan right there: 'I poured Guinness over me cousin. Pure. Irish. Erotica.' It's no mystery. US-based Gay.com and UK-based Gaydar.ie, where gay men can order up sex like pizza, have eaten up that market.

Gaydar is more popular in Ireland as it's more user-friendly. In fact, ordering up sex is probably easier than ordering pizza.

Here's a real-time snippet from users in the main 'Eire' chat room window:

'Anyone at all here from Limerick city?'

'Anyone looking to meet? Southside.'

'Any guys in Cork?'

'Married for same.'

'Anyone looking to meet northside?'

'Twenty-one-year-old, hung, fit, student, looking to meet with under-thirties guy near D11/D9, anyone? Before I do myself damage...' That last one sounds like a threat.

Despite all the technological advances, we are back where we started: sitting opposite another human being who is just as nervous, just as wanting and just as lonely as ourselves. We can become anything we want online, embellish the truth, seek out adventure. But when we pull the plug and get ready for our date we are back to where we started: a pot belly and crow's-feet.

THE MAN WITHOUT A FACE #1
They met online and, after some sexy chat, exchanged photographs. He was dressed in a tuxedo. It looked like he was strolling – or, as she says, 'striding' – down the red carpet at the Oscars.

It was very James Bond, she says. The Bond from the book, not the film. The unknowable, mysterious, untouchable Bond. The secret of his success was that she couldn't make out his identity. That's what, privately, she liked about his photograph. It fuelled her fantasies. It gave her hope.

His suit was single-breasted and fitted him well. She could only see his jawline. Nothing else of his face was visible. From this angle, it looked like a strong, square jaw. His face was brown, probably tanned from the LA sun. And that walk. Beneath that well-fitting suit lay the hard body of a hard man. Somebody worth winning over. She liked that he lived in Dublin and she in Cork. The distance made the meeting more worthwhile.

She, Catherine, was forty and beautiful. But she was tall, maybe 5'9' or even 5'11' in heels, and she had the kind of face that grows from pretty to handsome. She was the kind of woman who would look better in her sixties than a woman in her twenties. People had compared her to Kristin Scott Thomas. There are worse actresses she could be compared to but it was becoming old-hat now.

She had tried and failed to meet the right man. One profile for a man in his fifties described a person who was honest without being rude, direct without being mean. Then in block capitals he stated: 'I detest cheating and cheaters…recently devastated by cheats!' Catherine says, 'He had more baggage than a Louis Vuitton factory.'

Another profile by Joe45 went on for about two thousand words, a mini-autobiography. He had played sports since his youth, believed he looked like George Clooney and listed every country he travelled to.

Catherine says, 'Joe reminded me of a golden retriever, bouncing and sniffing, pausing long enough only to admire his reflection in a puddle before dashing off to chase another stick.'

Plenty of others seemed emotionally stable but ended with inflammatory statements like: 'No head-wreckers need apply!' Or, 'No fatties! No offence!'

Before 007, Catherine had also met quite a few loop-the-loops. 'Percival was a silver-tongued eccentric who loved wordplay,' she sighs. 'His profile had a lunatic ring to it but he used words so beautifully that it was beguiling.'

Percival told Catherine he was forty and he was rather vague about what he did for a living. 'We decided to meet in Fitzgerald's Park in Cork,' she recalls. 'It poured with rain – we're talking monsoon weather. He couldn't find the right gate and it took us an hour-and-a-half to find each other. He looked a bit like a ruined Bryan Ferry. An extremely wet, ruined Bryan Ferry.'

He didn't have Bryan Ferry's money, style or musical talent. In fact, he didn't even have his own place. 'He lived in a room in a house nearby,' Catherine says. 'Actually he lived in half of the room – it was divided in half by a red curtain and a family lived in the other half. He even showed me their pictures.'

'Percival invented children's games for a living but in twenty years he'd never sold one. He was so broke that I paid for his cup of tea. He insisted that we drink it outside in the rain because take-away was cheaper than sitting in the cafeteria.'

007 would be a step up. This time would be different. Wouldn't it? She ran through her photographs. The holiday shots in her bikini were too presumptuous, too forward. She didn't want him to think that they were going to have sex. She hadn't slept with that many men in her life. Not counting the ones she didn't want to remember, anyway. They were meeting for a drink in McSorley's in Ranelagh. She was in Dublin on business.

What she looks like naked is hardly relevant. He'd sent her a secondary picture of himself on holidays, leaning against a signpost on Rodeo Drive, of all places. He was wearing a sun hat and shades. She couldn't make his face out. 'I wished he hadn't sent it,' she says. 'It spoiled the James Bond image.'

He travels. So what? Doesn't everyone these days. She picked a photograph from 2003. Or was it before that? She hadn't changed much since then, anyway. It was only five years ago. This would be a date she'd remember. Or, put another way, it would be one she would never forget.

MASTER MANIPULATOR
'My boyfriend chatted to me anonymously online.'

Hi Q
I met my boyfriend of two-and-a-half years online.
We don't live near each other. Last year he bought

me a PC for my birthday and I started logging on again on my Internet profile. Turns out, he has been in my email and logging on to chat to me as a different user.

I lied about it simply because I knew he wouldn't like it. He says the trust is gone now and that he could trust me as a friend but not trust me in a relationship. All I did was talk to complete strangers. I did not meet them. He also has a female friend. He says they're just friends.

We don't live near each other but he tells me that he doesn't know what he wants any more. He has told me that he loves me and thinks the world of me...yet can't go out with me.

Why is it one rule for him and another for me? Do I have a right to be angry about what he did? Is it possible to stay friends?

'All Over the Place'

Dear All Over

I don't know whether he had an ulterior motive when he bought you that computer but it seems that he has used this as evidence against you in order to break up, a decision that was already made. This way, he has the moral high ground and all the cards and he is taking his time deciding if he wants to scale down the relationship, continue or just be friends, while pursuing his options.

It's clear he still likes to string you along. It's not important whether I think it's over or not. It's more important to deal with the facts. Everything points to it being over, or close to, yet you appear to be quite capable of convincing yourself that it could be salvaged in two years' time. For what it's worth, the relationship, as you know it, appears to be over. You should prepare to accept it.

IN THE BLEAK MIDWEEK #1

The pub near Dublin's Temple Bar is nearly empty. This is Quiet Wednesday, one of MaybeFriends.com's weekly social gatherings. This is where, according to the radio advertisements, this website will give you the 'hottest social life in town', change your life from 'boring to electric' and 'change your maybes into definitelys.' That offer seems too good to resist.

MaybeFriends.com is more than just a dating website: it specialises in social networking, getting people away from their computers into the real world, with special meet-and-greet events held by Jill, who manages the website. Quiet Wednesday is their signature night out.

Facebook is a forum to show off your many fabulous friends but what if life and other circumstances beyond your control have conspired against you? Quiet Wednesday is the place to go.

On this particular night Sam28 is presiding over the evening. She has thick, chestnut-brown hair, which falls straight just below her shoulders. She has a robust figure and a round, smiling face. She giggles animatedly, the giggles of someone who was once shy. She is the organising force behind Quiet Wednesday.

It's not that unusual for someone to loiter at the entrance of the bar or even sit at the bar and have a pint, partly scoping the group out to make sure they're not a crowd of misfits...and partly hoping that someone will spot them, ease the transition and bring them to the rest of the group. Me included.

Two of the guys and one girl look at me, suspiciously. In order to dispel any sense that I'm a voyeur, I announce that I too have a MaybeFriends.com profile: Parismatch. That does the trick. One has a problem with me being there but warms up when I explain, 'No guns!' and 'No names!'

There may no longer be a taboo about having dates that originate online but there is still a taboo about making friends online. Nobody likes to admit that they've reached a point in their life where they don't have anyone to go to the movies with or have lunch with on a Saturday afternoon. These are little things we take for granted.

But if you're in your thirties or forties and your friends have got married, and you're single or separated or divorced or married to your job, you might find yourself suddenly cut adrift from the social life you knew when you had the time, money and energy to hang out in nightclubs. And now? You don't want to feel like the lump in the corner.

'I joined because I had no friends basically!' says Sam28.

You have to admire her honesty.

Sam28 has worked for more than four years as an office administrator, with one boss and no colleagues, so there is no social life there. 'It's just me and my boss, so I can be in 'chat' while I'm at work. I was so bored doing nothing, not going out. I lost contact with my school and college friends. I studied business, secretarial skills and accounting in Ballsbridge. Other students got married or just wanted to be married.'

'I'm so glad I joined. I never realised how many friends I could actually have. It's amazing.' She adds: 'There are even a few I'd call my brothers.' She sits on a high stool with her pint of water. She – wisely, considering this is a school night – doesn't drink. She tells me why she found herself without a social life. 'Before, I thought I could have only one friend,' she explains.

This is puzzling. What on earth would stop her?

'I was afraid to let people down,' Sam28 adds. 'One friend wants to go to one place and the other person wants to go somewhere else. Now, I don't feel that because they're all going to the same place.'

She effectively put all her social eggs into one basket. Surely she can please herself, spend time with two friends on one night, allow friends to go somewhere they choose without feeling responsible – or even just go ahead and please herself, without that being a guilty pleasure? 'I didn't want to let people down,' she says again, still smiling.

The blue light on her phone keeps flashing as more members arrive, over a dozen by now. She checks her phone with the seasoned professionalism of a nightclub-owner or a wedding-planner. The evening is picking up.

There's a lot of buzz about a recent pay-in social event. 'There is a civil war on the message board. Have you seen it?' Sam28 asks, as if it was the latest plot twist in an online soap opera. It is a disagreement arising from a recent charity event.

In a country with the youngest population per capita in Europe, this group shows you can work, shop, go to Mass, go to college, go home…yet still be totally alone. Maybe people now wonder, at the tail-end of the economic boom, what it was all for?

There are two new arrivals. Sam25 – this Sam is male and is the one who set up Quiet Wednesdays – and his fiancée Freckles are a big, cuddly couple: rosy cheeks and a youthful blush. They are inseparable. They've had a roller-coaster courtship: they first met at a Quiet Wednesday a few months ago and they have been inseparable ever since. They're back tonight to celebrate their relationship.

Sam25 wears a navy-blue windbreaker and keeps pulling his jumper around his mouth. He's not feeling well but didn't want to miss tonight. He rolls back on forth on his heels.

Freckles is lively, has long brown hair, a round face and a girlish pale-blue jumper. She's called Freckles for a reason. 'I've got millions of freckles and I always hoped they'd join up and form a tan,' she says. It's the first of many first jokes. They are a couple who like to joke and if you don't like their jokes – believe me – you won't like this couple.

She also has a sister from Saggart in tow, who is not a member of MaybeFriends.com. She looks uncomfortable.

Sam28, tonight's hostess, Sam25 and his fiancée Freckles are like family now, they inform me more than once. They greet each other like characters in an Australian soap opera, as 'brother' or 'sister'. It doesn't help that their profile names are both Sam. And they're not actually related.

Sam28 is single on this night. She doesn't know it yet but she will find her heart's desire. For Sam25 and Freckles, despite their punchlines, it will all go horribly wrong.

FROM STONY GROUND...
'Nobody knows I met my girlfriend online!'

> Dear Q
> My girlfriend and I have been together for almost a year. For the first time in my life I know I am really in love and we are very happy – we both feel that this could be it. But we actually met on the Internet and nobody knows this except us. I guess

we were too embarrassed to tell anyone at first but now it's just gone on so long that our friends might be offended if we told them that we'd kept it from them for this length of time.

You see, neither of us would classify ourselves as the type of person who'd go looking for their partner online. But it just so happened that we'd both signed up to the same dating site for a laugh, never expecting anything to come of it. Sometimes, I feel like a big fraud when people ask me how we met and I reel off the standard 'eyes meeting across a crowded pub' story.

I'm afraid that people will think less of our relationship if they know how it really began. Should we come clean and risk the ridicule, or should we just let things lie and keep our secret to ourselves? My girlfriend jokes that she's going to stand up at our wedding and give everyone a surprise by telling them how we really met. But I'd rather it didn't come to that. Help!

'Internet Shame'

Dear Shame
You didn't meet in a noisy bar after you'd both had too much to drink? Mutual friends didn't organise an awkward dinner party because they felt sorry for you? You met on the Internet? That's just about the most romantic thing I've heard all day. A true 21st-century romance. No bar-room noise, no alcohol, no meddling? Just two brave souls floating out there in the world, reaching out into the digital

void that is cyberspace. I'm loving your girlfriend's impromptu wedding speech already.

It sounds like a pretty good start to me. There are many respectable, fun, online personal sites out there.

From stony ground, your relationship grew – strong and vibrant. You did well. Be proud of the fact that you tried something new, put yourself out there. It's more than a lot of folk do, believe me.

THE MISSIONARY AND THE SUPERHERO #1

Orla loves Jesus. For the longest time, she wasn't sure if she needed another man in her life. But then she met her husband Dan, a former superhero and mild-mannered one-time TV weatherman from Dallas, Texas. He too loves Jesus, so they were well matched. As orthodox Catholics, they are not the likeliest of couples to have hooked up on the Internet, that hell-hole of pornography and late-night booty calls.

But their relationship is testament to the fact that there's something for everyone on the Web: they met – drum-roll, please, *as we give it up for Jesus!* – on AveMariaSingles.com. Even the wholesome MaybeFriends.com has some wily folk looking for threesomes. Not here. On this website, people are not even looking for sex. Not off the bat, anyway.

The site asks questions like: Are you committed to finding the one? Are you practising your faith? Are you able to marry in the Church? Are you opposed to using contraception? Are you open to wherever that right person is? Do you believe God can really use this site?

It advises:

Our members are typically Catholics who love the Church and believe 100 per cent of what the church teaches. They are practising their faith in their daily lives and seek to meet someone of the same conviction. We are not saying that these are 'perfect' people or 'saints'. They are sinners like we all are. But our members truly care about their journey toward Christ and a life in Him…

Orla, a former missionary from Derry, and Dan don't believe in sex before marriage, contraception, divorce – the works. And, unlike many Catholics, they actually practise what they preach. She *is* comely. She's tall, slim, has shoulder-length brown hair with some high- and low-lights, creamy skin from all that healthy living and is radiant and calm.

As a youth, Dan was a blond, square-jawed, handsome American jock. He's a little more portly now but he's still got his all-American hair and chubby cheeks with a ruddy glow.

Dan worked as a TV weatherman for five years in Jackson, Mississippi. But while working in radio he had an alter ego that was bound to be attractive to any woman: 'Super Dan.' He would squeeze into a pair of tights and a red cape and fly around Dallas with a mobile phone, making people's dreams come true or doing crazy stunts to promote the radio station.

'It was one of my first jobs in radio almost fifteen years ago,' Dan says. 'I worked for one of the morning shows. For example, I asked women what they'd do for George Michael tickets. I started that gig during the first Gulf War. I sat on a billboard waving an American flag and people would honk their horn.'

Today, he is plain Dan with a multi-million dollar wish to get the first Catholic radio station in Dallas on the air. 'There's a lot of Protestant radio stations in Dallas,' he says.

It's not often you get to meet such a holy Trinity: (a) an orthodox Catholic; (b) a superhero; and (c) a wireless disciple of the word of Christ. But with the help of her spiritual adviser and passages from the Bible, Orla met a three-in-one.

Before she met Dan, Orla was working as a missionary in Holland. She was burnt out, so she took a sabbatical and moved home to Derry for the summer. 'I felt I should be married but thought I'd be single for the Lord if that's what He wanted,' she says. 'There was never desperation to be married, I was very content. It seemed ridiculous. When I saw other couples, I didn't have that active yearning.'

She originally studied physiotherapy in London for four years but these were her wilderness years. 'I got a bit wayward when I went to college,' she says. 'I was in more liberal circles. I won't go into details but my moral life declined and I was guilt-ridden over a lot of things. I was attending church but I was resisting the Lord.'

That was all about to change, which is where the Internet came in. When a relationship in London broke up, Orla turned back to Catholicism: 'I came to fall in love with God in a way that I hadn't known before. I just wanted to give him my life. I wanted to do something more specifically for the Lord. I found God was leading me out of physiotherapy. Patients were talking to me about faith issues. They had this terrible resentment and sadness towards God, as they wanted to be as they were before.'

Orla moved to Dublin for eight months to take up Catholic missions training, was sent to India for a few months and ended up in Holland, where she lived for four-and-a-half years. But she was unsettled and while she was doing research on the Internet, she saw the light of her computer screen promote a site called

AveMariaSingles.com. 'It was under Our Lady's patronage,' she says. 'The Pope was put there as a supporter of it.'

When Orla's personal ad went live in Dublin, Dan was already live in Texas, after his engagement to an American girl went south in 2002. 'I picked Holland,' he says. Where the girls are tall, leggy and blonde. He's a Catholic, after all, he's not dead. He sent out two emails, one of which was to Orla, and he held his breath.

NUMBER ONE
'His ex is Number 3 on his Bebo list.'

> Dear Q
>
> My boyfriend and I have been going out for a few months and we're very serious. He left his long-term girlfriend to be with me. He was out of love with her for a long time before he ended it. Anyway, he still has her as a friend on Bebo. In fact, it wasn't until I asked that he placed me before her and removed all the pictures of them. He didn't seem to pick up on how inappropriate and inconsiderate that is. How can someone tell you that you're the love of their life and simultaneously have their ex prioritised over you on their social network device? By the way, we're in our twenties…just in case you thought we were teenagers from the mention of Bebo. Should I insist he move her down the line? She's his Number 3 friend at the moment.
>
> 'Angry'

Dear Angry

You're in a relationship, not in the CIA. All this Internet monitoring has got to stop. You've asked him to remove the pictures and re-prioritise. That's as it is. The inappropriateness and inconsiderateness of the situation are – for the most part – in direct proportion to your anger and sensitivity. You change one, you change the other. I suggest starting with the latter two first.

You can ask him to delete her as a friend, move her further down altogether, to Number 20 or 40 or 60 or 600. But you can't really control somebody's feelings about the past and you can't rewrite it.

A strong, independent and self-confident girlfriend trumps any ex-girlfriend. It certainly trumps a girlfriend who may want to rewrite the past but cannot. Wouldn't you prefer his past not to be hidden away somewhere and for it to be up-front on his Bebo site at Number 3, while you reign supreme at Number 1?

Isn't his past better there, out in the open, where you can see it?

THE MAN WITHOUT A FACE #2

On a rainy night, Catherine met 'James'. Alas, he was no 007. Like Sean Connery under the toupee, he was bald. Except he had no toupee. His head glistened under the lights in McSorley's of Ranelagh. Like a new penny.

Many bald men are sexy. Hot as Hades. 'He wasn't one of them,' Catherine says. 'It was his manner more than his head. He was nothing like he appeared to be in his picture,' she says.

But wasn't his face obscured in both pictures? What the blazes did she expect to waltz through the door? 'Yes, but if that was the reason he cut the photograph off at the nose, he should have told me. That's what put me off. I felt cheated.'

As for him, he never said she looked older than her photograph but he never said she looked younger either. He studied her for a moment when he met her. 'He stared, more like it,' she says. It was a look that was full of hard questions.

She felt the cool glare of his gaze. She scanned his face for disappointment. 'I told him I was thirty-eight,' she says, unapologetically. 'I look good for my age.' And she does.

She didn't sleep with him. Not right away. 'I would have felt like a hooker meeting in the bar of a hotel,' she says.

He lived nearby. He invited her back for a drink. She hardly knew him. But she was lonely and a few drinks took the sheen off his forehead. Most of her friends are married. When she gets home at seven in the evening, she's wrecked. She makes dinner and turns on the television. 'Being away from home,' she says, 'I felt free.' So she said she would go home with him. Just for coffee.

And how was it? Fireworks? Testosterone? You know what they say about bald men. They're burning on all cylinders.

'He couldn't get it up,' she says. 'Maybe it was the wine or the pressure. It happens a lot on the first night.' He did, finally, but it was…

'Just okay. There was too much expectation.' And too little time? 'Maybe. I'm not sure we would have gone on a second date, even if I hadn't slept with him on the first night.' So why did she? 'Because maybe he wanted to sleep with me. It felt good to be wanted. I remembered how his pictures made me feel. Maybe I wanted to sleep with my original idea of him.'

Why not leave after the first drink? Or, if that seemed too rude, after the second. 'I was there and I'd spent hours speaking to him online. I was only in Dublin for one night, so it was him or nothing.'

Catherine did something before she left, a small, silent act of rebellion. 'I opened his bathroom cabinet and there was a dusty bottle of Rogaine.' She drew a big exclamation mark on it. With her index finger. 'I feel ashamed now,' Catherine says. MaybeAshamed.com. Or MaybeIShouldFeelAshamedButIDon't. com. She was smiling when she told me.

She wanted James Bond. He wanted Kristin Scott Thomas, from *The English Patient*, not *Four Weddings and a Funeral*. That's what he told her when they originally corresponded. Even his fantasy was a complicated one. He wanted her to be fey, flirtatious. She wanted him to be strong, sexy. He wanted boobs and youth. She wanted him to be well-endowed and virile. It's not a lot to ask, is it?

And then – bang! – their fantasies collide.

Just like that, all the pent-up romantic expectation and sexual innuendo come to a head. In a super-pub in Ranelagh of all places, smelling of cleaning detergent and lager.

PANTS ON FIRE
'My husband looked at Internet porn and lied about it!'

Hi Qs
I'm married eight months and, up to last Sunday, was happily married. In the past, my husband and I had some problems because I found out he was telling me lies. Last Sunday, I discovered that he had been looking up porn on the Net. I challenged

him about it, he denied it and actually got really cross with me for accusing him. I knew it was him, so I pursued it. Later, I asked him to tell me the truth and not to lie in view of our history with his lies. He sat me down and I asked him to look me in the eye and swear that he didn't do it…and he did just that.

Later that day and many shouting matches later he admitted that it was him. He only came clean to save himself embarrassment because I said I was going to ask his family if they'd been looking at that site.

My main concern is that he lied to me. He looked me in the eye and lied. When this happened in the past, we agreed to move on. But I said if he ever did it again, I'd never trust him again and I might even leave him. He agreed that I'd be right to do so. In my heart, I know that if we weren't married I'd probably have left him by now. I feel that marriage is built on trust and that has now been ruined.

'A Worried Wife'

Dear Worried
Mindful of your opinion on porn, your husband chose to lie. Perhaps he felt ashamed. Perhaps he felt like a chastened schoolboy caught in the act. He was certainly treated like one. Or perhaps he knew how it would make you feel – insecure about your relationship and yourself – and wanted to spare you that.

No doubt there are some husbands out there who don't surf the Net, looking for porn. While they do exist, I don't believe they're exactly thriving as a breed.

Marriage is a serious commitment. But it should also be an enjoyable one. I'm saddened to hear you believe you have a 'history of lies' after just eight months. The problem here lies with your ability to trust...perhaps because your husband has given you fair reason not to trust him.

You are treating your marriage like a precious, perfect piece of art. But rather than bathing in its beauty, you are scouring it for imperfections. The closer you look, the less precious it becomes. I don't believe we should become blasé about telling lies. But you are his wife, not his Sunday School teacher. Are you in love with him? If so, remind yourself and your husband of that and of all the wonderful reasons you got married in the first place. Marriage is based on trust. You say he has lied before. It is important to distinguish the white lies from the serious ones. Otherwise your growing fear of losing him could well become a self-fulfilling prophecy.

IN THE BLEAK MIDWEEK #2

'Hello, brother,' says Sam28.

'Hello, sister,' Sam25 replies.

It's confusing. And it's not because Sam28 is a girl and Sam25 is a boy but they're both called Sam. It's because they are *not* related. 'She is like my sister,' Sam25 tells me, referring to Sam28. Freckles, his fiancée, smiles. They're all smiling at one another.

Back at the MaybeFriends.com's Quiet Wednesday, it's difficult to keep track. Who is dating whom. And who isn't related to whom. Classifying friendships as siblingesque relationships gives them intimacy and also bestows security on them. It's more difficult to drop or fizzle out a friend you've called 'sister' or 'brother'.

This group values the security that brotherly or sisterly friendship brings. Sam25 and Freckles, for instance, weren't about to dilly-dally in shacking up. 'We met on the first Quiet Wednesday and were living together by the second,' says Sam25.

I hold, then bite my tongue.

Freckles invokes the hands of the gods: 'It was like something else took over.' I fear her concept of fate comes from watching too many blockbuster DVDs. But perhaps it gave her the courage and security to feel they're doing the right thing.

There are many well-rehearsed lines that sum up their relationship and capture the magic. *Lake Placid* was the first movie they *ever* watched together. And then there are the necessary soap opera suds, gleaned from a thousand TV romances.

'My sister-in-law suggested that I get a pre-nup,' Freckles says, while her sister from Saggart rolls her eyes in sympathy. Why? 'Because he's on a winner,' Freckles adds, echoing her aunt's dark thoughts. (Freckles owns a house in the ex-burbs of Celbridge.) 'But as far as I'm concerned, I'm the one on a winner.' Another well-rehearsed line. Ba-boom!

I can't help wondering if Sam25 feels emasculated by all this talk of pre-nups. If he is, there's no sign of it. He is still bobbing up and down on his heels, as if to say, 'No problem here.'

They craft the story of their Internet love around the soap opera model. But as all soap opera viewers know, the happier you are and the louder you declare your love, the more likely the hands of the gods (or script writers/producers) will bitch-slap you when you least expect it.

Sam25's chirpiness doesn't waver. He tells me the secret to this relationship success. 'You've got to get out there,' he says.

The secret is not as profound as I would have liked but I don't doubt it.

Meanwhile, Freckles's Sister from Saggart is a case in point. She cut out the Internet middleman and, with her sister, came straight here to Quiet Wednesday in search, perhaps, of her own Prince Charming. Freckles's sister seems uneasy.

Freckles understands: 'It's a long time since you've been in town,' she tells her.

Sam25 is used to this kind of small-talk and banter. When we meet, he is working in a camera shop in Tallaght.

Freckles, meanwhile, threw herself into a career 'to break the back of the first three years of the mortgage'. She's worked with those suffering from Asperger's syndrome, in the tourist industry, as a life-skills instructor and with prisoners. And then…'I went online and I've never looked back,' Freckles says.

'You were wearing a neck brace!' her fiancé Sam25 quips.

Freckles cracks up. In fact, since she met Sam25, Freckles says she has never stopped laughing. 'My jaws were sore. You know when you get that lockjaw?' Not apart from tetanus, but I nod. And Freckles starts guffawing all over again.

And they all lived happily ever after. Just not with each other…As it turns out, Freckles didn't need a pre-nup, after all.

Several months after this Quiet Wednesday, the laughter had stopped. As had the one-liners. Sam25 claims he had twenty-four hours to pack his bags and leave Freckles's house in Celbridge. He says Freckles called all the shots. She says there were more serious problems in the relationship.

'She'd cancelled the venue for the reception, the Royal Dublin Hotel on O'Connell Street, before talking to me,' Sam25 says. 'She was used to being entirely responsible for her own life. I think relationships are about sacrifice and benefit. She had to be very strong and tough to be where she was. She thought that was appropriate in a relationship as well.'

He adds, 'She wanted to keep the ring but I took it back. I know how to fuss over someone and put them on a pedestal and make them feel special. I expect one week in four at least to decide where to spend our weekends. Quiet Wednesday has given me a fair bit of inspiration since the break-up.'

Freckles may have stopped laughing when they broke up, but she started again when I called her up and told her Sam25's version of events.

'It's not true that I gave him twenty-four hours notice. It's funny how people have different stories,' she says. 'I wanted to postpone the date, as I thought it was too soon. He moved out. We'd been discussing this for three months and he didn't move out until the third month. I wouldn't have made any sort of commitment if I didn't love him. I have contacted him a couple of times. I didn't hear any response or comment. He decided to cut ties. I've moved on and put it behind me.'

Meanwhile Sam28 kept on organising Quiet Wednesdays and kept her positive outlook. It paid off. She met a man at a Quiet Wednesday and became one of the eighty-plus MaybeFriends.com marriages. She dropped off the message boards and stopped coming to Quiet Wednesdays soon after. Another satisfied customer.

Sam28 sent me a message online before finally disappearing from the virtual world. 'I found someone and couldn't be happier.' That was the last I ever heard from her.

I did wonder what it's like to be in a state of mind where it is impossible to be any happier than you already are. Is it like sitting on the top of a ferris-wheel with a big stick of candy floss, destined never to get off, a kind of emotional immortality? Whatever it feels like, I wish her well.

Quiet Wednesdays fell off the radar too after Sam28's departure. Jill, manager of the site, asked Delboy2712, an amiable Dubliner, to revive them. Delboy2712 was a good choice. He had once dated Sam28 before she left the site and met her husband.

He breathed new life into Quiet Wednesdays. In the Mercantile Bar on Dame Street. He puts a message online saying he'll be wearing a lilac striped shirt. He's easy to spot. It's the only one in the bar. But just like last time, I had to be greeted at the door.

The next generation of MaybeFrienders are just as hopeful as the last. A group in their thirties and forties, some singletons, some single parents, some who gave their time to their jobs or their children and found their friends from their twenties had got married and moved on. Like the old group, they are close-knit.

Alan42 is a case in point. He worked unsociable hours in the off-licence trade, then realised work had taken over his life. He changed jobs, now sells mobile phones and broadband and decided to set up a profile. He chose a moniker simple and to the point: Alan42. Although he's now forty-three. That's what happens when you put a number in your profile name. You get older and, like Dorian Gray, your profile stays the same. He has grey spiky hair and a stocky build.

Alan42 seems almost too nice for this world. But he's in good hands here.

'I nearly had a heart attack when I got my first email,' he says. 'Walking into Quiet Wednesday was the scariest thing I've ever done in my life and I've done some scary things. I was feeling down in myself. I had low self-esteem. I was lonely.'

Alan42's neighbour saw his profile online and gave him a bit of a slagging. It didn't occur to his neighbour that in order to see his profile, he had to be online too. Alan42 finds women friends are better than men. 'Men don't talk about how you're feeling. They talk about soccer and sex.'

He's been on a few dates. All went well. None of them turned into anything romantic. He has no regrets and, he says, hooking up with Quiet Wednesday was the best thing he ever did.

A recent evening ended up in the Viper Room. 'I was eating a hot dog at three o'clock in the morning on O'Connell Street,' he says. 'It was like being a teenager again. I love Quiet Wednesdays. In life it's important to have something to look forward to.'

Sam28, the High Priestess of Quiet Wednesdays, would be proud.

UP CLOSE AND PERSONAL
'My online personal ad needs some oomph!'

> Dear Q
> I've tried pretty much everything to meet the right man. After a few bad – and some good – experiences, I've decided to set up my own personal ad. I sound corny and every time I want to write something real about myself I get writer's block. I don't want to sound dry and boring. My writing

skills need a little oomph! I'd enlist the help of my friends but this is something I wanted to do off my own bat. Any tips?
'Writer's Block'

Dear Writer
You're right: why not have the mountain come to Mohammed? Why spend weeks, months, years scouring the nightclubs of your own home-town when the country, nay the world, is your oyster? In fact, you can still scour the nightclubs while your own personal ad is working its magic 24/7 like fly paper.

The first thing you've done already. You're looking for a relationship, first and foremost. Now that you've decided that, specify it in your ad. Online dating, like real-time dating, is more miss than hit. So here you get to: (a) attract the right type; and (b) check their profile is compatible.

For what it's worth, here are my top ten tips:

1. Don't try to be funny, if you don't feel funny.
2. Don't let the website tie you into a small-minded straitjacket. Salary details are tacky.
3. Employ the same care you would for your CV. You don't have to be Margaret Atwood or Edna O'Brien to spell-check. One domesticated lady I found asks to be 'sweeped' off her feet. Will this romantic act involve a broom?
4. Avoid mealy-mouthed gripes about exes. One forty-something guy wrote, 'Anything

unhygienic, picking certain parts of the anatomy really annoys me.'

5. Feel free to specify age, looks and the kind of qualities you find attractive. Go beyond the GSOH level.

6. Don't fall into the faux-modest: 'My friends thing I'm good-looking.'

7. It doesn't hurt to say you're happy if you're happy, you're sometimes lonely if you're sometimes lonely.

8. If writing isn't your cup of tea, say so. One guy says he is 'a lousy speler (sic) with a vibrant and slightly odd sense of humour'.

9. Uploading a photograph helps. Call it direct marketing but it works. Post the good but no airbrushing.

10. When asked where he'd like to be, one guy wrote, 'In an open field surrounded by tornadoes that make my body sway to and fro.'

Be evocative, be personal, be bold, be safe.

THE MISSIONARY AND THE SUPERHERO #2
Dan got two responses to his emails. The first girl was too busy but says she'd get back. The other was Orla, who had been working in Holland as a missionary.

'She wrote me that December,' Dan says. 'I'd never talked to anybody internationally before. I bought a calling card. We spoke the following January for the first time.'

Dan, who was studying theology part-time at the University

of Dallas, offered to help her find a Catholic college in the US to attend.

When they swapped photographs, Orla included one of herself as maid of honour at her sister Mary's wedding and plenty more with children from her missionary work.

'She was beautiful, very pure and elegant looking,' Dan recalls. 'What attracted me most was that we both take our faith very seriously and that her whole life was devoted to spreading the word of God.'

'A lot of pictures she sent me were her with children,' he adds. 'She obviously had a maternal side, which was good as well. She sent her life story, the good, the bad and the ugly…her early struggles. I knew pretty much everything about her past. Her pitfalls. Everything happened very quickly.'

Only months after the first emails were exchanged, Orla visited Dan in Dallas, staying at his sister's house for nine days.

She was thirty-one and Dan was thirty-six. But Dan didn't believe time was on their side. 'We weren't spring chickens,' he says, not just speaking for himself. 'We prayed about it and decided we were right for each other and that we'd get married. But we also decided she'd have to go back to Holland and talk to her spiritual adviser.'

Even before Dan had met Orla, he'd already told his sister that he was 90 per cent sure that he wanted to marry her but Orla had more soul-searching to do. 'She needed more word from the Lord,' Dan says.

She prayed for guidance. 'I asked Him, "Lord, I need to hear from you." He speaks to me through scripture. I had an impression to read a certain psalm and it says: don't be obstinate, don't be like a bull. I will take you and lead you by the hand. I don't actually hear an audible voice but I do recognise the peace that I get. And that's how God speaks to me, through my sense of peace.'

Orla's mother looked to the newspapers rather than the Bible. She asked, 'How do you know he's not a serial killer?' Fair comment but this question was regarded as an unnecessary worry rather than divine intervention. No one else resisted. Orla took that as her second sign.

In their wedding video, the couple sit in the door of a Rolls Royce on a windswept beach on the northern Irish coast. The camera sweeps and moves in for their close-up. They gaze into each other's eyes, holding glasses of champagne aloft. It reminds me of the girls from the 1930s who – to quote the song – stepped out of a dream. They smile, their lips quivering, swathed in freshly-pressed silk. The camera loves them.

Dan came clean during the speech at his wedding: 'Rick, my best man, told me there's this website I want you to look into…I joined that night. About two years later, I did my first international search…Orla is everything I looked for in a wife. When I see Orla, I see the face of God.'

You can't say better than that.

'She sincerely loves Jesus,' Dan says. 'She brings me to a new plane in so many ways. I pray more. I say the Rosary more. I iron my underwear! Why God picked me I'll never know.'

The website is devoted to those who are devoted to their religion. 'There are a lot of questions on the website,' Dan says, sitting in their cosy, immaculately-kept apartment in the suburbs of Dallas. 'How often you go to Mass and what you think about abortion, divorce and contraception.'

'Contraception,' Orla adds, 'is still a no-no. It's a lack of understanding about where those teachings come from. John Paul II's teachings on the theology of the body will blow you away.

If you read them, you'd never be pro-choice. You'd understand how contraception would never be allowed in a healthy marriage relationship. It's not a full gift of self to each other and that's how God intends it to be. I have been in relationships where it hasn't been like that. I see that living like this is much more precious.'

Ten months after their wedding, Lily May was born.

Orla is still acclimatising to her new home in Texas. 'Dallas is very flat and doesn't have the rural beauty of Ireland, which I miss a lot,' she says. 'We have to take day trips to places like Oklahoma, which keeps me satisfied.' About the Internet, she has a less spiritual, more pragmatic, parting shot. 'It saved us from meeting at Starbucks.' And with the price of coffee there, it's probably just as well.

2

The Sexual Devolution

It used to be so simple. Boy meets girl in a dance hall, they go out for a year, maybe two, they get married, have children and everyone lives happily ever after with their bunk beds and station wagons and nobody missing the absence of under-floor heating and en suite bathrooms.

Forty years ago, if you were single after thirty, you were the exception rather than the rule. The most glamorous job in the country for a woman then was to be an air hostess with Aer Lingus. A single woman who is thirty today has less in common with her mother than possibly any other generation, so fast has society changed.

This has led to a regressive cultural phenomenon, the sexual devolution. All deals are off. Booty calls might be fun if you're twenty-five but are they still fun when you are thirty-five? Do you take the chance that he/she will still want you in the morning? From this stony ground will something tall and proud grow?

How did it come to this? The Americans manage to date several people at the same time, they break bread with a number of possible life partners until they make a formal declaration to commit. Here, dinner-dating is virtually extinct. It's a few dirty great pints and back to your place.

If some men have brass balls, and think they have time

and power on their side, there are women with ovaries of steel, who are bolder and stronger. Alcohol helps, of course, but bar-room Barbarellas hunt men as aggressively as their mothers were courted. Men drink for Dutch courage, just enough to get them over the finish line. Studies on erectile dysfunction say that it's not just men of a certain age who have problems in this department. There is increasing pressure for men to perform, to live up to their bravado.

'If I hear the line "I have a lot on my mind" from a man one more time...' Mary, a twenty-eight-year-old receptionist, says. On Mary's last date, the man forgot his wallet, then asked if he could take the receipt to claim the money back on expenses.

Not all women see the sexual devolution as a bad thing. Sally sleeps with men and leaves them crying for their mammy. She's not hard-hearted. She is free. She wants boyfriends and good times, not a long-term relationship. Not yet. 'My womb is not a void that needs to be filled. My womb is also a source of creativity and strength.'

There are no rules for dating any more. Because there is no dating culture. It's an asphalt jungle out there. Don't believe anything your parents told you about courtship and romance. Men are taking back in the bedroom the power they lost in the boardroom.

Welcome to Ireland's dating season where men and women do the walk of shame as the sun comes up over the wreckage of the city after Saturday night. It was fun. A night to remember. Wasn't it?

THE EMPIRE LINES STRIKE BACK #1
Anna has just turned forty. She lives on the first floor of a house in Blackrock, overlooking the sea. You can see the little yellow

lights on the Howth peninsula as they curve their way along the edge of the water. They twinkle like little jewels in the night.

'It's like a necklace,' she says, sitting on the steps of the Georgian house, smoking a cigarette and sipping a glass of wine. She has red, shoulder-length hair, combed back off her face. She doesn't wear much make-up, nor does she need to.

If that glittering skyline is a necklace, Anna bought it herself. She pays her own way in life. She has never married. She is too long in the tooth to give up her freedom at this stage. Does she want children? Maybe before. Not now.

Perhaps it's the years of putting up with men who have pulled one stunt after another. Or maybe it happens to us all when we reach our forties. Either way, I wouldn't mess with her. As for dishing the poop on the men in her life. She. Is. Ready.

Anna's best friend Emily, an archivist, is less forthright when it comes to men. At least, she used to be. She is about five years younger than Anne, petite with jet-black hair and a fringe almost covering her long eyelashes. She has a wardrobe full of empire-line dresses, which she usually teams with hoop earrings and high heels. Jane Austen is one of her heroines, but that's more a coincidence. She just likes the look.

Anna's flatmate, Jason, who is thirty-six and a music promoter, loves listening to their dates from hell. He steps out of the doorway, all dickied up like a dog's dinner. He knows Anna is disillusioned with men. Irishmen. But he believes that one half of her loves the drama.

'There should be a Sid and Nancy aspect to every relationship,' he says, 'especially in the first few weeks. I am completely faithful when I'm in a relationship and a slut when I'm not. Hedonism and monogamy are not mutually exclusive.'

He's off on a date with a Swedish girl.

'I tell my friends, typical middle-class Irish blokes, that I'm dating her and they turn into these pirates. They say, "Ooo-eeer! You're dating a twenty-nine-year-old Scando-bird. Ooo-eeer! Can she bend over and touch her toes?" That's a middle-class Irishman's fantasy.'

'Have a nice time,' Anna says, throwing her eyes up to heaven and returning indoors with her glass of wine.

Jason is half-way down the garden path but turns for a parting shot. 'For the record, I love Irish women,' he says. 'But I am very sceptical about their attitude to one another. Irish women do not like to be introduced to one another, especially by a man.'

If that's true, Emily and Anna are the exception. They bonded during the 1990s and shared romantic adversity. Like when Anna finally broke up with her on-again/off-again boyfriend Bernard, an insurance salesman from her London office but who spent months at a time in Dublin. He rented a place in Ranelagh.

He was known as 'Bernard Mustn't Grumble' because that was his favourite phrase and the philosophy by which he lived his life. He wasn't a complainer. He spoke in a very slow, deep Cockney drawl.

Picture it: Ranelagh. 2006. Bernard Mustn't Grumble invited Anna and Emily for dinner. It would be the last time either of them would see him. As Emily, the third wheel, recalls, 'I was only there for the free wine.'

Bernard explained the reason for his surprise return.

'The only reason I came back to Dublin,' he told them, opening the second bottle of wine before dinner, 'was the hope that Anna and I would get back together.'

'Feck off!' Anna said and went outside for a cigarette.

'More wine?' Emily asked.

Bernard said, 'I have a vintage bottle of port but…'

They opened it.

As Anna had her cigarette outside on the patio, Bernard asked Emily: 'What about it?'

'About what?' Emily said, looking around.

'You and me?'

Emily poured herself another glass of vintage port. After the first, she was outraged. After the second, she was perplexed. And after the third...'I thought it was funny,' Emily says.

He may have lost Anna but Bernard, living up to his name, wasn't going to grumble.

Bernard stalked her for three months. 'I still get texts from him at 3 am,' Emily says. 'He knew I wasn't into him but he also knew I was too polite to tell him.'

The men they met were never what they appeared to be. It was like a hall of mirrors.

A perfect example is when Anna met a blond bombshell after her Christmas party. He was gorgeous: tall, slim for a man in his thirties, polite, sensitive. He worked out but was toned rather than over-developed. He had a stomach as flat as a washboard. Even his fingernails were clean. 'He was dressed beautifully,' Anna says, 'I couldn't wait to get him into bed.'

She went back to his apartment in Leopardstown.

'My bedroom is a mess,' he said. 'Let's stay in my sister's room, she's away.' So they did. They slept in a bedroom with pink frills, sparkly jewellery, flowery dresses and feather boas.

The next morning she woke with a hangover.

He told her, 'I work in MTV.'

'MTV? As a presenter?' she asked him.

'I'm on the TV,' he said. Or what she thought she heard.

'RTÉ?' she asked again.

'No,' he replied for the third time. 'I said this is not my sister's bedroom. This is my bedroom. I'm a TV!'

Now she was really confused. 'You're a TV? You mean you're on TV? You want to watch the TV? You work for MTV?'

He said it for her very slowly. He lifted up one of the dresses. It was nice, she thought, a floral Laura Ashley number, a bit fussy for her taste.

'These are my clothes. I'm a TV,' he said one final time.

She looked around. The large dresses, the even larger bras and the even larger high-heeled shoes. This was one big sister. 'I guess I just thought she was big-boned,' Anna recalls. But as she continued the scan the room, it made sense: the padding drooping out of one drawer, the oversized costume jewellery, the ultra-feminine room, the lack of tampons when she rifled through the bathroom cabinet the night before to see if he was on any medication.

'A TV?' she said. Finally the first ball dropped, then the second one.

'A TV,' he repeated, seeing the recognition flicker across her face, 'a transvestite.'

'Oh,' Anna said. 'I see…'

Did she mind?

'No,' Anna says, 'he was great in bed, so sensitive and caring and giving. It was the best sex I'd had in ages. He was a generous lover. He listened to her when she spoke. He was the first man she had met who had impeccable manners, the one exception being the white lie that it was his 'sister's bedroom'. To quote Tootsie, he was proud and lucky and strong enough to be the woman that was the best part of his manhood and the best part of himself.

Some time passed. Anna's flatmate, Jason, had his car burnt out by his ex-girlfriend. She went on a date with a Garda and they had sex in his garda car at Sandymount Strand. When she was late for work one morning, he got her there in eight minutes flat using his siren. For Anna, it was business as usual.

Fast forward to 2008. Anna was single again. Emily and Anna were attending a wedding reception at the Four Seasons in Ballsbridge and Niall, a guest at the wedding, asked Anna if she wanted to share a taxi home.

'I had too much to drink, wobbling all over the gaff, and I was ready to leave,' Anna says.

Niall was going to Dalkey. She was off to Dún Laoghaire. They could split the difference.

'He gave me the glad eye,' Anna says. 'I wasn't interested.'

Clearly he was. Because the taxi went neither to Dún Laoghaire nor to Dalkey. To Anna's surprise, when she opened her eyes from her drunken daze, it had arrived at his house in Milltown. Turns out, they lived nowhere near each other.

'I said, "One drink, and I'm going home," Anna recalls. 'I realise it was a stupid thing to do but I was plastered.' She kicked off her kitten heels, which were killing her, and curled up on the sofa.

'You won't be going anywhere,' Niall told her, 'I've hidden your shoes.' And he went to bed. Expecting Anna to follow him. Talk about buttering a cat's paws so it wouldn't find its way home.

'They weren't Manolo Blahniks or Jimmy Choos but I loved those shoes,' Anna says. 'I tore the place apart looking for them.' Finally, she gave up. She kissed her shoes goodbye, walked outside and flagged a taxi barefoot. 'It was the only time in my life I was shoeless as well as legless.'

FISTFUL OF NUTS
'My girlfriend abuses me in front of our friends!'

Dear Q

I have been with my girlfriend for four months. I am madly in love with her but she does the most hurtful things and does not seem even to care. She is insecure and has been separated from her husband for two years. She has her own home and car and wants for nothing. But she seems to be taking something out on me and I don't know why. For example, I got her beautiful jewellery for Christmas and she got me nothing. She said she didn't have time. Yet, she got something for her whole family, even something for her ex-husband.

On New Year's Eve, in front of all my friends, she humiliated me. She was sitting on a friend's lap. For no reason, she picked up a fistful of nuts and threw them in my face. I said nothing, just got up and left the room. The next morning, when I challenged her over it, she said that she didn't remember, told me to 'get a life' and ignored me.

What's going on? She says she loves me. The other night, she had a few drinks and texted me to say how bad she is to me, that she does not deserve me and I should get someone better.

I don't want to break up as I do love her. But I just don't know what else I can do.

'Emotionally Bruised'

Dear Bruised

She is not someone who is ready to have a relationship.

You love her, she's breaking your heart, humiliates you in public, says she's sorry, storms off, flies into a rage, texts you to say she thinks you deserve better, excludes you from her Christmas list... and so it continues. Her drunken moments of repentance are not enough to keep this relationship afloat.

This is an awful lot of misery to cram into four months. I think if a really nice girl came along (and she will) you would soon question the love you have for your current girlfriend. Sometimes, we confuse the desire to be loved with the love of someone who is entirely unsuitable.

Recounting all the times she (and/or you) have acted badly will not make things right. You are just reliving this nightmare and punishing yourself. She's not showing you respect or love. Forget about her. The fistful of nuts should have been the wake-up call that you needed.

Don't wait for this girl to have a personality transplant. She won't. You can't change her. Stop waiting for her to show you respect. By walking away, that is something that you can easily give yourself.

THE MEN WHO KNEW TOO MUCH #1

Timothy is a thirty-something serial monogamist. As he peruses the menu in Bobo's burger joint on Camden Street, he admits that his last girlfriend broke him in. They dated for five years. They butted heads about music, film, theatre, books and politics. Theirs was a nourishing, sometimes tempestuous relationship. She single-handedly turned him into the perfectly faithful, well-balanced boyfriend.

Then they broke up.

Suzie forced him to deal with 'stuff'. Stuff like? 'Emotional wellbeing,' he says, 'hopes and dreams.'

She liked to talk about where the relationship was going, why they should spend X amount of time together and Y amount of time apart. Now he can't stop talking. The result? Few girls, if any, will have revenge fantasies about him.

'Even now when I meet women I hate small talk,' he says. 'I just want to get straight into all the heavy shit. At first I found the introspection very wearing but then I really got into it. There's no point in resisting the Talk. Most men have a real horror of the Talk.'

He cites holidays, weekends away, nights out with the lads as housekeeping that should be sorted early in a relationship. Plus how much of yourself you should commit to the relationship and how much of yourself you keep independent, because everyone needs both elements. 'That's all time-management and boundaries,' he says.

Timothy won't talk about his ex-girlfriend, his family, his flings – not in a way that would break a confidence or seem boastful. He is keenly aware of those invisible, precious boundaries all around him.

Because Suzie broke him in, his relationship with Amanda, his current girlfriend of one year, has more emotional clarity. He is fully evolved, more than many men of thirty-eight. With his easy manner, blonde spiky hair, strong physique and healthy appetite – although he orders the 'Ranelagh' veggie burger with falafel because it's Monday – he is proof that nice guys do exist.

He is rarely long between girlfriends. When he is single, he does enjoy his life but he never remains in that place of bed-hopping for long. He enjoys the dynamics in a relationship too much.

Timothy was a moody, broody teenager. 'I was angry,' he says. 'But I think most Irishmen have very poor self-knowledge. They don't tend to understand their emotions, why they are the way they are, or their sexuality. There were no forums to discuss them when I was a teenager. I was very envious of girls who had that social network growing up. Men can't have that support network for a lot of reasons.'

Girls can get close physically and emotionally but it's too gay if men do it, unless it's on the rugby pitch in Castleknock and there are lots of mud and hot showers involved.

'You are so self-conscious as a male teenager, you don't even have the vocabulary to deal with your emotional life, never mind the inclination,' Timothy says.

But he didn't learn everything he knows from Suzie. Timothy brought something valuable to both his big relationships, with Suzie and Amanda. 'I think men bring a sense of perspective,' he says. 'Around 50 per cent of women's issues are valid and need to be discussed and the other 50 per cent are bullshit.'

'Here's an example. I recently worked in an office with a girl who was dating a guy for a couple of months. They hadn't officially told people they were a couple, she still wasn't calling him her "boyfriend". Anyway, she had a row with him about his not coming out to meet her. The women in the office turned into a lynch mob, chanting, "Dump him! Dump him!" Turns out he was at a family gathering and didn't want to leave, which is not so bad. Sometimes that female support network can make matters worse. They're not distinguishing between the real problems and the trivial bullshit. It all gets equal weight, which it shouldn't.'

Timothy has met Emily and Anna. He knows them socially. He likes Emily a lot and, for a while, thought about asking her out on a date but: (a) he had met Amanda a few days earlier and, although nothing happened, he had a feeling about her; and (b) he respected Emily and knew that if he was to ask her out and she said yes, he would have to be fairly serious about it. And he wasn't ready. 'I took six months out between my last two relationships. I needed that time to get over them.'

He enjoyed those six months. 'Your thirties is also a great time to be single. You know who you are and what you want. You can date women in their twenties without feeling like a perve but you can also date divorcees in their fifties, plus all the women closer to your own age.'

Ah, yes. Each time Timothy meets a new woman it's like he has his first kiss all over again. 'Like the smell of a new car,' he says, smiling sheepishly, 'and the smell of the leather. But I know that it isn't something you can do for ever. The male sex drive can take you places you really don't want to be. You don't want to be one of these toxic bachelors who prey on women's emotional needs in order to get laid.'

Which is why he never stays single for long.

He does not believe men should take girls to the pub on a first date. 'I think dinner is always good. You go on dates with people you like and people you've talked to, people you know. If you don't think you will get along over dinner, you shouldn't be alone with them.'

Why do women like Emily and Anna have such a hard time with the blokes they meet? Speak, Timothy…

'Some women wake up at the age of thirty-four and think, "Omigod! I need a man." Naturally they want children but they have spent all that time trading in derivatives or sending out press releases. Relationships don't get built in a day and we live in a culture of instant gratification. To get to that place where you want to make a lifetime commitment can take a long time. I read a study that said that the women who find husbands aren't the best-looking or most submissive; they are the most decisive. They look at a man and say, 'That's for me. I'm going to make this work.' I think many do want loyalty, appreciation, love, respect and affection before children and marriage, and I think it should be in that general order.'

Nor does he pretend to understand women. He had one brief entanglement with a girl who broke up with him. He wasn't exactly devastated. He reserves that adjective for civilisations that are washed away by tsunamis, earthquakes and flash floods. He took the break-up in his stride. 'She actually gave out hell to me for not being more upset that she was breaking up with me,' he says, 'which I thought was pretty funny.'

So what makes his current relationship work so well? 'We're from different worlds so we're not competitive and we're not competing for the same airtime in the relationship. I'm in the media. Amanda is a doctor. We come from two very cliquey professions. I'm really in love but it's not that nauseous feeling I got when I was twenty-five. That kind of obsessive love is not a good thing. Men can so easily become unhealthily obsessed with a woman. I'm not sure why that is.'

Does he like being in a relationship? 'Yes, I do, but it can be hard work. One of the best things that it does is stop that accretion of selfishness that goes on as life goes by, where it's harder to break your habits and accommodate someone else in your life. I understand that it would be a hugely generous act for anyone to marry and give themselves over to another human being.'

There's an added advantage. 'My mother is giving me all these hints along the lines of: "I think she could be the one." '

What is it about mothers and sons that is so important? 'I'll tell you why: because the thought of your wife and your mother not getting along is truly frightening.' Does that make him a mammy's boy or a smart boy? Probably a little bit of both.

FUNNY LADY
'I told my boyfriend I missed two periods as an April Fool.'

Dear Q

I took last April fool as my last chance to play a really big prank on my friends and gorgeous boyfriend. I told them my period was two months late. Everyone, including my boyfriend, was very supportive. And, of course, my friends were really pissed off when I told them the truth. My boyfriend, on the other hand, was okay with it, or so it seemed.

Since then, I have noticed that I seem to be the one who calls him, and I sense something's gone from our previous situation. I knew the joke was risky but I also thought he would be relieved and happy to hear it wasn't real. Have I ruined the best relationship I've ever had? How do you think I can make it up to him?

'Jokester'

Dear Jokester

This doesn't sound like an April fool. It sounds like a test disguised as an April fool, which is probably why your boyfriend has cooled. And understandably so. I say this not to chastise you further but to help you understand why he might be annoyed, aside from the emotionally trying minutes/hours he had to endure, thinking he had a baby on the way, and why you chose this as an April fool.

You need to honestly ask yourself why you picked such a cockamamie April fool joke (was it the humour or were you really curious to see how he'd react?) and grovel like you've never grovelled before. Explain how silly and reckless the joke was and – if you do find any other reasons why you decided on this one – tell him too. Be honest with him and yourself. And be contrite.

WHAT'S SEX GOT TO DO WITH IT? #1

Paisley is the girl who has everything. Or almost everything.

A quirky, funny personality, beautiful looks, a grand turn-of-the-century house overlooking the sea in Howth at the tender age of thirty, a red BMW sportscar to fly around in, her own advertising business and a collection of truly loyal friends, male and female.

Some of her male friends have become lovers briefly but they always went back to being friends. She would never have known had she not tried. And Paisley does try.

Take Ciaran. It was her sixth date with him. On the first, second, third, fourth, fifth dates, he said all the right things. He had studied psychology, which Paisley thought gave him an empathy, as he said all the right things.

'I can't believe how lucky I am to have met you,' Ciaran told her. 'You are a beautiful girl, you're funny, you're independent, you have your own house, your own business…'

He may have studied psychology but on their sixth date, Paisley said he was less 'ology' and more 'psycho'…

Paisley was seven minutes late. She got three messages and a voicemail asking where she was. That's one message for every 1.75 minutes. He had a face like thunder when she arrived but she talked him down and the date went ahead.

With hindsight she sees how vulnerable she had become. 'He had asked me so many personal details about myself that it was only later that I realised he wasn't interested in gradually getting to know me, he was trying to do what Jack Nicholson did in *The Shining*: he wanted to break down the door with a psychological sledge hammer. I told him a lot about my life because I didn't want him to think that I was not able to open up. I thought he was a decent guy and I didn't want to lose him.'

He viewed her Facebook profile between the fifth and sixth dates. He quizzed her over the photographs. He told her she was unladylike in a few. Her concerns were like parking tickets: she filed them away in a drawer and ignored them. 'I'd only known him a couple of weeks but I decided to make the best out of a bad situation.'

Ciaran revealed more about himself too. 'My ex-girlfriend tried to kill herself when we broke up,' he said. He wore that information as a badge of honour.

He added, 'I had a one-night stand and have a ten-year-old child. I have to pay the mother €60 a week. She tricked me into it. I have enough financial pressures without that.'

Armed with that information, they went for dinner in L'Gueuleton, a French restaurant on Fade Street, where he hummed and hawed about the bill, pushing it in Paisley's direction. She had one starter and a glass of wine; he had three dishes and the best part of a bottle, followed by a dessert wine.

Ciaran finally relented. 'You can get the first two rounds,' he replied.

They decamped to Lillies. And ordered a bottle of champagne. Paisley paid. 'I didn't want him to think I was cheap,' she says.

His friend Luke arrived.

'He must really like you if he bought champagne,' Luke said.

Paisley bit her lip. Ciaran reluctantly admitted that he hadn't put his hand in his pocket. Luke and Ciaran loudly debated whether they should buy another bottle or a glass. Paisley offered to chip in. They said don't be silly, then went halvies… on a glass.

An hour later, they kissed. During their embrace, he said, 'Do you shave down there?'

She assumed he was joking and replied, 'It grows down to my knees and I French-plait it twice a week.' With that, she stood up to leave.

'Are you manipulating me by going home?' Ciaran asked.

Paisley felt bad. Maybe she'd been too hasty. She asked him if he would go out for a cigarette. When they went outside Ciaran finally told her, 'I don't fancy you. It's over.'

'Listen here Mr €60-a-Week Child Maintenance, Don't Want to See Your Child, Don't Want to Buy a Bottle of Champagne, Your Girlfriend Tried to Kill Herself…' And then she really let him have it.

Like I said, Paisley does try. She does not lack hope. Her well of hope is replenished time after time. After time. There was one problem, however. She still had not met the right man. Any man. She had other needs too. She hadn't had sex in one year. 'Actually,' she says, 'make that two.'

And so Paisley went speed-dating. She had a double tick with one guy she did want to see again. He ticked her box. She ticked his. He signed himself 'Mike'. She would later call him: 'The Farter Who Refused to Go Home'.

They met a week later in her local. He talked about himself non-stop but, like the sands in the hourglass, the bottle of wine they were sharing was almost empty. As they poured their two last glasses, Mike said, 'It's your round, let's get another bottle.'

'I'm not one to welch on a round,' Paisley says (Ciaran can attest to that). So she agreed.

At closing time, Mike offered to walk her home. When they got to her front door he said, 'Can I come in for a cup of coffee?' She didn't want him to. She wanted to get rid of him. She wanted the night to be over, so she said…'Yes. I said, "Yes."' Why? 'I know it sounds weird but out of politeness.'

Paisley did something incredibly naïve. She let Mike in. He sat down in the living room. She went into the kitchen to make the coffee. She was taking him at his word. 'When I came back into the room with the coffee, the stench was unbelievable,' she says. 'He had been farting like crazy. I held my breath and tactfully opened the windows.'

She sat down and he went in for a snog. 'I thought, "If I give him a quick snog, maybe he'll go."' During the snog he broke wind again. This time, it was a high-pitched squeak.

'My dog probably heard it in his sleep,' she says.

Mike said, 'Your walls look like they need paint-stripping and I thought I'd oblige.'

Paisley had had enough. She said she was tired and he should go. And, miraculously, he did. Five minutes later the doorbell rang. It was Mike. 'I've lost my keys,' he said. 'Can I come in and stay?'

Paisley said no.

He put his foot in the door and said he was not leaving.

She let him in…out of politeness. As long as Paisley could maintain an air of normality, everything would be okay.

'I'll sleep on the couch,' Mike told her, 'I'll be gone in the morning.' The next morning, he was.

'After that, I got an alarm and a phone in my room. And yes, I stopped doing things out of politeness.'

A couple of weeks later, she decided to meet Damien, another speed-date bump, for drinks. They went dancing in Renards and left together. He was cute and she decided to bring him home.

He whispered sweet nothings into her ear all the way home. When they got there, she took him to bed. It was all so romantic. Like a Mills and Boon. Damien whispered compliments into her ear, how he desired her, wanted her, needed her. After a build-up that dignified her two-year wait, they were under the covers. That's when he whispered the whisper of all whispers: 'You want my balls slapping up against your backside, bitch?'

'I wasn't used to one-night stands,' Paisley says, 'and I was already a little nervous. But I couldn't go on. I started laughing. I said, "Where did you get a line like that from?"'

'A porn movie,' Damien said. 'I've always wanted to use it.'

Did she kick him out of bed for bad dialogue?

'No. I thought, "In for a penny, in for a pound" – if we'd gone that far already we might as well continue.'

Damien asked her for a hairbrush. 'I want to slap the back of your ass with the hairbrush,' he said.

'I didn't know how one-night stands worked,' Paisley recalls.
'I thought, "It's weird but… why not?"'

And that's when Damien chased Paisley around the bed with
the hairbrush.

She did learn one valuable lesson from both her dates:
'Never, ever do something out of politeness.' And: 'Posh boys
think they're in a porn movie but they end up like caricatures
from a *Carry On*.'

PET PEEVES
'Can you imagine waking up next to a dead gekko?'

> Dear Q
> I have been dating a nice guy for a couple of years
> but a few things are starting to bother me.
>
> He hasn't bought any new clothes for himself
> since I've known him, although he's a merchant
> banker and can easily afford it. Yet he lavishes
> designer stuff on me that I never want and have no
> intention of wearing.
>
> His foreplay technique is lacking, to say the
> least. It consists of him getting an erection and
> thwonging it into the small of my back at about
> 3 am.
>
> His pet gekko is allowed to sleep in the bed
> between us! Actually, this is gekko number two
> as the first one suffocated! Can you imagine what
> it's like waking up next to a dead gekko? Am I
> being difficult or are my complaints justified? Best
> wishes.
> 'Girl from Cork'

Dear Girl from Cork

I guess many people could say they've woken up next to a few rats in their time – but a pet gekko?

The clothes issue is minor. Sit him down and say to him, 'Although I appreciate the gesture, I don't need you to buy me clothes. Why don't we go shopping together, instead, and buy you some things? You haven't bought clothes in years and I hate to see you get neglected!' Tell him that he has a good eye but you have your own style.

As for the foreplay, that's a major issue. You have to be careful as you don't want to damage his ego or dampen his spirits. You could play hide-and-seek or go clothes-shopping for sexy underwear. Bottom line, you've got to make him aware that a thwong/thwong here and a thwong/thwong there, here a thwong, there a thwong, everywhere a thwong/thwong do not constitute foreplay.

The best sex comes from being able to speak up, as well as get it up *before* you hit the sack. And the gekko has got to go-go.

THE EMPIRE LINES STRIKE BACK #2

It was the date from hell. Literally. Emily and Anna, best friends and partners in crime, were in La Cave, the basement wine bar on South Anne Street in Dublin, having a drink.

They got chatting to a group of oddballs, some of whom were fun, but Emily wanted to fly the coop. Just as she did with Bernard, Anna slipped one of them Emily's number.

'I thought he was a bit creepy,' Emily said the next day.

'How can you be sure?' Anna said. 'Odd men work harder for

it. And anyway, give him a chance and don't be so shallow.'

The creep, whom we shall call Heston after his favourite chef, turned out not to be so creepy. Not at first, anyway. He sent her texts like: 'Lovely Emily, how are you?'

She felt she could get used to this.

The effusive texts kept coming. Then one Friday night: 'Lovely Emily. I'm at a film festival all weekend but I'd love to escape for a while.'

Emily wondered if he was a writer, director, producer, actor. Or all the above. She thought, 'Maybe I'll give him a chance.' And she did.

They met at 6 pm outside the Irish Film Centre. 'It's not like it was outside the Savoy,' she says. 'I'm thinking arts and culture. So I rock up to the IFI and see a big poster saying, 'Horrorthon Weekend'. Then I see Heston. He is a lot taller than I expected. About six-foot-three. I'm five-foot nothing. He is leaning against a Horrorthon poster like Lurch from *The Addams Family*.

'I'm thinking, "Shit!"'

'I've been at these horror movies all weekend as well,' he told her. 'I'm in a horror movie club. Do you know anyone in a horror movie club?'

Emily did not. She was not happy. 'I mean, this is the roughage end of the cultural food chain,' Emily recalls. 'I had this image of horror-movie buffs as the loners and the boners. I suggested we go to the Long Hall for a drink, somewhere public, well-lit. He started telling me about the different ways the girls get murdered. The safest thing to do was to find out if he had any friends.'

'I hang out with people from my horror-movie club,' he said. 'I had them over for dinner and cooked them a Heston Blumenthal spaghetti bolognese that took four days to make.

Just before I served it up, somebody tipped an ashtray into the pot.'

She asked if he knew who did such a terrible thing. 'I have my suspicions,' Heston said. His face darkened.

She tried to change the subject and asked him about his job. He worked as an engineer.

'Let me guess what you do for a living?' he asked, eyeing up her big hair and empire-line cleavage. 'You work in retail?'

'Uh-uh,' she replied.

'You're a hairdresser?'

'Uh-uh.' Wrong again.

This was not going well.

She told him she was a librarian who also worked as a freelance archivist. She loves books. She consumes them. *Pride and Prejudice*, of course, is one of her favourites. As is Donna Tartt's *The Secret History* and…on she went. She could talk about books to anyone, even Heston. He sat gazing at her, his face a blank.

Heston took her hand. 'I haven't been listening to a word you said because I can't stop drooling over you.'

Drooling? Did he say drooling?

She rapidly started yawning.

He was on to her. 'You don't want to go out with me, do you? I thought we'd catch a late movie at the Horrorthon: *For Your Height Only*.'

Emily is five-foot-two in heels. And there was a midget in the title role.

She left.

On Hallowe'en night, three days later, she received her final text from Heston. It read: 'Be careful if you go out tonight because the pretty girls always get murdered first.'

Emily went back to dating men who are tall, good-looking and with impeccable manners…on the first couple of dates at least.

The farmer was a case in point. She and Anna were having drinks outside Kehoe's when Emily overheard his conversation.

'I'll go and try my chances with that blonde,' he said.

As he passed, Emily said, 'Good luck!'

'You've chatted me up,' he said. 'I'm staying here.'

Paddy was all man: meaty arms, veins protruding from workouts, a handsome face, thick brown curls, tanned. He looked like a Calvin Klein model with a Cork accent. 'I've dated some cute men,' Emily says, 'but the farmer was the dog's bollox.'

They went back to Emily's house near Baggot Street. Everything was going well. This would be the first of many dates. There were, however, signs that all was not as it should be, which she tried to ignore.

A voluptuous female nude hangs over her fireplace. Paddy looked up at it and said, 'She must be Irish because look at the shanks on her!'

That was how it would continue. They would walk down Grafton Street and Paddy would say, 'Look at the size of her ass.' Every woman should be like a hanger. No woman could be too thin. Nor did Paddy like eating out. And he was very set in his ways. 'Don't expect me to bring you to restaurants because I won't bring you,' he told her. 'I don't do texting either,' Paddy said. 'You can text me but don't expect me to text you back.'

Emily hung in there for a month. Like Paisley, more parking tickets in the glove compartment. 'He invited me to Cork for the weekend,' Emily says. 'I bought a pair of pink floral Wellington boots in Avoca for the occasion. I was so excited. For dinner he made carrot and celery salad.'

She tried to make it right in her mind's eye as they walked the land of his country estate. His family lived in the main house. They were staying in one of the gate-lodges. She could move from Dublin for this. She could be mistress of his domain. It was all so perfect. In Emily's Jane Austen version of events.

On the Friday night they had sex. How was it? 'Amazing!' Emily said.

On the Saturday afternoon, there was farm work to be done. 'I had to go out and count the heifers. Every time I went near one they went "Urrr!" with disapproval. The heifers were so mean to me. I thought, "Why can't the heifers be nice to me? Even they don't like me." The heifers wanted Paddy for themselves. Women are always so hard on other women.'

That night, they ate another salad – broccoli and celery – and drank a bottle of wine. Maybe it was the heifers outside, mooing loudly throughout and making their disapproval heard that their master had a female guest, but there was little body contact and more heated conversation.

Paddy gave more of his opinions about women and the way they might look at you. 'All Irish women are fat and not a bit stylish,' he said. Emily tried to fly the flag for the sisterhood. But it was no good.

Fast-forward to the bedroom. Paddy sat up. 'Are we getting divorced?' Emily was surprised. She knew things weren't going well but well, he was so hot. 'We obviously don't get along,' he added.

For the first time in her life, Emily lost it with a man. 'Why did you let me drink the wine if you knew you wanted to break up? Now I'm stuck in the middle of nowhere.'

It was a bollocking that would have silenced the heifers as well as the lambs. They were quiet by now. Emily reckons they had shimmied up to the house and were all listening.

She lay in bed waiting for first light, texting Anna the whole story. At 6 am, her idyll was over. There was nothing more to say. Without a word, she got dressed and packed her things.

She trudged across the gravel in her heels, got into her car and left, leaving the Calvin Klein farmer standing in his jockeys in the doorway. But she did not look back as she rumbled down the driveway to the main gates. She beeped her horn at the triumphant heifers on the way out.

DUST BUSTED
'I do all the housework and cooking. He works late.'

> Dear Q
> I am in a relationship with my partner for fifteen months. He moved into my apartment after four months together. I work in a nine-to-five job but his job is far from that. He can leave the house very early and not get back until 8.30-9.30 in the evening. I do love him very much and he tells me often that he loves me and I'm the best thing to happen to him.
>
> We're both in our late thirties and have a history. However, while I think he does love me I feel he does not get involved very much in our relationship. At home the cooking/shopping and housekeeping are left up to me. He uses the excuse of his long hours and I always feel sorry for him. When it comes to organising our social life that's left up to me too.
>
> How do we get past this place we are stuck at? I

feel so frustrated at times but I don't want to sound like a nag. I do sometimes wonder if he's taking advantage and having been hurt several times in the past I do not want to be made a fool of now.

I also have to say that we are total opposites. I am a perfectionist – not good I know – and like to get things done now. He is very laid-back, sometimes too much so, I think. I have tried to discuss these issues with him and he apologises and says he loves me and he will change. I suppose my big question is: do I continue on even though I know he won't really change and just accept it? No one is perfect after all.

'The Housekeeper'

Dear Housekeeper

Many couples have somebody who is the better cook or who enjoys it and somebody else who may do the housework and/or grocery shopping. This really is a housekeeping issue, both literally and metaphorically, although statistically women usually do more of it.

If your partner gets home late, maybe it's not so easy for him to cook during the week. I suggest making one mid-week evening his cooking day but keep it flexible, as you don't want it to turn into a chicken bone of contention if he calls to say he's held up. I also suggest thst he cooks at weekends and gives you those off. If he's too busy during the week, fair is fair. If he does a nice tomato sauce or soup make it a habit to do more than you need, so you can freeze it and have it a couple of days later.

Ditto the housework. Make a plan, ascribe times to do certain chores and make it clear that it's better to have a routine for shared responsibilities because it removes the arguments. You both sign up to it at times when you're free and it makes it easier for you to stick to it.

Timetables are a way of taking the issues and drama out of your relationship and on to a piece of paper that is stuck to the fridge with a magnet. It's as simple as that. When you live with someone, you need to approach the housekeeping and bills in a regimented fashion, just as you would with office work.

On a personality level, you are the high-maintenance one, he is the low-maintenance one. It's good to bring that to the table, too. To acknowledge it. It's not bad, it just is what it is. After the honeymoon period is over in a relationship, couples are faced with two main conundrums: the 'issues' (in this case, the housework) and the 'personalities', how the differences between you become more apparent the longer you stay together.

You can't change your personalities but you can put in place a strategy that helps to minimise the conflict that those differences cause.

THE MEN WHO KNEW TOO MUCH #2

Sean, a forty-something serial singleton, is a clear ten years older than Timothy, the thirty-something serial monogamist. Sean thinks they should meet. 'I was him ten years ago,' Sean says. But contrary to popular belief about the male of the species, he is just as introspective as Timothy, just as self-analytical, just as much in touch with his feelings, the choices he has made, what women want…and what men want in return.

He is more cautious than Timothy. And Timothy is cautious. Sean is intensely private – and rightly so. He hasn't got to where he is today – still single – by treating his life as an open book.

Sean has a girlfriend, Emma, a writer like him. But 'I won't be asking my girlfriend to marry me any time soon,' he says.

He has had six serious relationships in his life. 'No,' he says, 'make that five.' What happened to the sixth? 'She just got downgraded.' (You can't see the raised eyebrow in print.)

The longest was four years but he is that rare beast, the exotic creature you don't see carousing nightclubs in the early hours. Sean is a writer, a thinker, an observer and content to be alone. He is the forty-something serial singleton, after all. Catch him if you can.

'How many forty-eight-year-olds do you see carousing in clubs anyway?'

More than he might expect.

He does not look unlike Timothy. They both have blonde hair: Sean's is flecked with grey, while Timothy's is short and spiked, Sean's is longer, more unkempt, fitting for a writer, a public display of his independence. There is no woman who would see it as her place to tell him to smarten up and cut it.

What makes him special? He's not the cad you heard about, the men Emily and her best friend Anna or Paisley have met in their search for the One. Yet he is doggedly single.

He is a nice guy. I tell him so. The words are only out of my mouth when I know to tell him that was a bad idea.

'I am outraged and insulted that I would be considered a nice guy,' Sean says.

Why? Does it make him less of a man to be a nice guy?

'Everyone knows that women run things, are clever and have more of an emotional range. To be a nice guy indicates that you are in some way subservient. Women let the man think he is in charge. They think, "He will do my bidding and change for me." They think they can tame men. To be a "nice guy" is to somehow collude in that.'

So women are like driving instructors when it comes to men and their emotions? 'They put the man in the driver's seat,' Sean says. 'Yet they maintain a pair of pedals, accelerator and brake, at their own feet…to control things when they see fit? I have found in my relationships that some women try to do that. The best option is to take turns driving. But some women will wrest the wheel from the man at inopportune moments.'

Such as? 'I had a girlfriend I was going out with for a short time. We had the "We Need to Talk" conversation. I said, "This isn't working." She said, "We both have to want to stop." I found that quite alarming.'

Given this story and his reaction to my 'nice guy' faux pas, does he fear entrapment? 'I am a single man in my forties who has yet to get married so yes, you might be right.'

But what about Emma? 'My current girlfriend lives in a separate country.' That's not an ideal situation for a relationship, surely. 'One postcode away is optimum.'

Is his lifelong struggle to remain independent more to do with his profession than with his sex? Do Sean and his girlfriend need space to be alone with their thoughts and to write?

'A friend of mine suggested a stable, ordinary woman would be a perfect foil for me.' How does he define that? 'Mary from the midlands who works in a bank.' Mary from the midlands who works in the bank is probably a holy terror when she closes her till and hits the town. 'Maybe you're right but it's unlikely I'll meet her. The only time I ever go to the bank is to ask them not to foreclose on me.'

That would explain why 'Mary' – wherever she may be – has never slipped him her number.

Sean is done with bolts of lightening. 'Every time I've had that, when I've walked into a room and the hairs stood up on the back of my neck, it's been tremendously exciting…electric. But it burns out. I'm interested in other kinds of women, people not like me. I think that feeling is narcissistic and happens when you meet someone just like you. You love them but you can't stand them either.'

Flaws, he says, are not seeing the difference between coercion and compromise, like always spending time with people you don't want to spend time with. 'Domestic issues. Younger women are mad keen about going to a nightclub. It's a number of years since that particular issue has raised its head.' Is that a good thing or a bad thing? Again a smile. 'There are still plenty of younger women who don't want to go to nightclubs.'

And what about opposites? 'Opposites do attract but they don't bond permanently. They bind and repel, bind and repel.'

'That famous feminist Sharon Stone once said a woman can fake an orgasm but a man can fake an entire relationship.' Has he? 'I couldn't possibly answer that. There are times when you go through the motions.'

I'm not sure whether we're talking about the orgasm or the relationship. I assume both.

Sean adds, 'Women think they have a monopoly on the former. With condoms it's also possible for men to fake orgasms.'

Men get headaches too, you know.

What if it works out with Emma, if he realises he can make this one work? 'In that case, I'd happily marry but not live in the same house. Or I'd get a big suburban house and we could each take a floor.' Finally, they would be living under the same roof. Sean thinks on that some more and pulls back a little. 'Or two houses connected by a door.'

Where does this caution come from? Is it male instinct or was it learnt? Sean thinks about that one but doesn't answer. Were his parents happy? That's the real question.

'I know,' he says. He doesn't answer it. More caution.

I have a question. He straightens up. It's a question that might offend. He is all ears. It is a question women get asked all the time but men more rarely. Sean shuffles in his seat. Ready? He nods (impatiently). Why is he single?

'I'm not single.'

Legally, he is. Why has he remained unmarried, then?

'Through choice. Or maybe nobody will have me, maybe I'm not good enough…wait, that was a joke! Believing there is the One can promote an unhealthy level of dependence in a relationship.'

But plenty of people would like to meet someone, only don't. Is that not a lack of self-confidence? Or is it, in fact, too big a comfort zone?

'If anyone really wanted to be married,' Sean says, 'they would be married. The only answer to that question about being single is not that there is a lack of available men or women, or self-esteem, it's because they want to be.'

That was the big question. It was the last piece of ammunition in my canon. Sean is victorious. 'Is that the best you can come up with? Is that the scariest question you can ask me?'

Okay, then.

Has he ever not got it up?

'I'm a man,' he replies. That answers that then.

Isn't there another reason why we want to spend our life with another person? Something he may be aware of as a writer? Fiction or non-fiction, it's better with two people, preferably lovers, and you cannot have drama, a good story, without conflict. Plus, doesn't everyone want someone to live with and die with? Nobody wants to die alone.

'Everyone dies alone. That's not a good reason to be in a relationship.'

This is a man who wants to live alone too, which is his right. But he is not cut adrift at sea. Despite all his reticence and big-bang theories and independence, he hasn't given up on relationships. His current girlfriend may live in a land far away. For now. But this forty-something serial singleton is willing to give it a try.

UNTIL THEY'RE LEGALLY WED...
My boyfriend doesn't want sex before marriage.'

Dear Q

I have been with a wonderful guy for the past few months. From very early on, he told me he had slept with two of his previous girlfriends but regretted it as he is very religious and sees sex outside marriage as a sin so he did not want us to sleep together. I was surprised but I respect his beliefs. I assumed that while full sex was out of the question, some heavy petting wouldn't be a problem and there have been a few occasions where we have gone further than kissing in the heat of the moment.

However, I knew he felt guilty afterwards and when we spoke about it he confided that he believed all 'sexual touching' should be within the confines of marriage. I am reeling from this. I love him and know he loves me but I am finding this hard to deal with. Before you start thinking he is gay or not attracted to me, I know he is, as it is obvious he feels the temptation to go further too but he is strong enough to resist it.

My dilemma is what to do. I love him but can I really survive a celibate relationship? We share the most amazing kisses and the chemistry between us is unreal. I can't help but think how great it could be in bed together. I'm afraid sexual frustration will drive me to cheat on him just for some sexual gratification. I see sex as part of a healthy, loving relationship. But I love this guy very much. He really is like no other guy I've known.

Can our relationship survive or will I be driven slowly insane? Did people really manage to save sex for marriage in the old days and am I finding this so hard just because I am not a virgin?

'Frustrated'

Dear Frustrated

I respect his right to celibacy but it does seem more than a little vexing that he has slept with other girls in the past and is deciding only now that he won't go to bed till he's legally wed. What are the chances? Still, it's his choice and he's entitled to it.

Usually, in situations like this, couples compromise with – as you say – heavy petting…or even some light petting.

Short of telling him that there is nothing shameful about your love or sexual love or intimacy or being closer, I think you're in a bind. If it were the other way around, I would tell him the same thing, especially considering that men are traditionally regarded as the hunters.

Put a timeline on it. If there is progress on an emotional level, there must be progress on a romantic/practical level too. If you do decide to marry and you are sure he is the one for you, I suggest a short engagement.

WHAT'S SEX GOT TO DO WITH IT? #2

Paisley's sister Jane used to be a bad girl. While Paisley is polite to a fault and hopelessly idealistic, even when being chased around the bedroom by a man with a hairbrush, Jane, the elder, is bolder, more of a jet-setter.

She was a regular in Renards and the now defunct River Club, where the lawyers were famous for their pole-dancing escapades and where a furious Anna once gave a clip on the ear to a barrister who was slumped in a drunken heap over the table, telling him, 'Get up – you are a disgrace to your profession!' History didn't record his response.

Jane is blonde to Paisley's brunette, attractive like her sister and, while she made some bad choices in men, she has given as good as she got.

When she was in school, she was conservatively dressed, bespectacled, quiet, with a prettiness behind her glasses that she couldn't hide. A couple of swift drinks later, the glasses would come off and 'Plain Jane', as she liked to call herself, would be 'Calamity Jane', dancing on tables with the best of them.

A little like Supergirl before and after the transformation.

Now thirty-eight, Jane never married. But she is still hopeful. On the one hand, she reminisces about old boyfriends, like *really* old boyfriends. On the other, she chats to a strange man at the bar, forgetting she ever had heartburn. Plain Jane and Calamity Jane coexist, like twin sisters, each one finding the other equally amusing. One keeps the other in check, the other shows her twin sister how to throw up her heels and party.

When Paisley and Jane's g randmother from Tipperary was on her deathbed, family, friends and neighbours kept a bedside vigil, taking turns to be there to say the Rosary while she lay dying. Early one evening, Jane was kneeling on one side of her grandmother's bed, with her grandmother's cousin's nephew kneeling on the other side.

'I got the feeling he was looking at me between Hail Marys,' she says. 'I thought, "Am I imagining this?" '

She wasn't. When they'd finished a set of Hail Marys and Jane's grandmother lay semiconscious, he whispered into her ear, "You never told me your granddaughter was so attractive."

It was almost enough to bring her back to the land of the living…one last time. He had a reputation as a womaniser. He was not someone Jane's grandmother wanted to see court her granddaughter. He would be the last person she would choose.

'Of all the places to make a move…'

The night of the funeral, when she was intoxicated and filled with grief, he made his move. His big arms like legs of ham wrapped around her, he moved in. She woke up the next day in his bed.

'If I get €20,000 in the will,' he told Jane, 'I'll be happy.'

Wisely, Jane's grandmother left him nothing. Except, perhaps, a last flicker of disapproval. Jane went on a date with him. Did she break up with him because of the crack about the inheritance? 'No,' she says, 'we met for a weekend in the Clarence. He put his feet on the coffee table and he put his knife in his mouth.'

It's a start.

Jane's story is informative. Here was a man who saw what he wanted and went for it, regardless of the sensitivity of the situation. With one life to live, he did not let this opportunity pass him by. Now she knows. Had she not tried? 'I would have been left wondering.'

Jane had dated John, whom Paisley called John Player Blue because he was a player, had a mouth like a sewer…and he was bad for her health. He was tall, legs like tree trunks, and had a devilish air about him. She got him out of her life but she never did get over her addiction to him.

One evening Jane saw John in Renards. It was the 2 am call of the wild. She wanted him. How could she resist something, someone who was so bad for her? He nodded in her presence, asked her to come home with him, gave Jane the lights – the glad eye – as he left, slipped something in her pocket and sent her a text message to say, 'Come home with me, plz…'

But Jane was in Renards on a date. His name was Kevin. He was everything John was not. He was shorter. John was taller. He was balding while John had a crazy head of curly hair that looked like it hadn't been styled, cut or washed since the seventies. Kevin had a secure job in insurance that paid well. John was gigging with his band but doing more ligging than gigging these days.

The bottom line: Kevin was a nice bloke. John, if you talk to his ex-girlfriends, was not. The classic good guy versus the bad guy.

It was their first date, so Jane had no intention of sleeping with Kevin, not that night anyway. She had told Kevin she was staying in a friend's house in Barrow Street that night. Always the gentleman, he walked her home, kissed her at the garden gate like a teenager and wouldn't walk away until he saw her pull out the key and her let herself in.

Fast-forward two weeks later. Kevin and Jane had gone their separate ways. She had come clean to Kevin about her deception, admitting that it was John Player Blue's house she had gone back to.

Something changed in Kevin after that night. He realised that he was quite the catch. He shaved his head, wore sharp suits, grew stubble, moisturised, stopped drinking pints every other night after work, joined a gym and got his groove back.

He saw that he had something that women wanted – good looks, solid guy – and he had years of experience of being sensitive to women and knowing how to talk to them and stand up when they walked into a room, hold the door for them. He simply crossed over.

Jane, meanwhile, got her comeuppance. Jane and John got back together for a while but John soon completely lost the plot. He was drinking a lot, even for him. The last night Jane and John spent together was the final straw. When she woke up at 6 am, there was something wrong. The bed was warm. And damp.

John Player Blue, at forty years of age, had wet the bed.

Jane jumped out of bed screaming. Up until that moment, his scruffy, rock star ways were sexy. But this…

'I made him clean the sheets and take my mattress down

to the garden to be scrubbed and aired. But he was strangely unembarrassed. He called it "fire-trucking", an expression he'd picked up during his year in Australia.'

In the months that followed, the balance of power shifted back to Jane. John needed to know that Jane wanted him. When she no longer cared for John Player Blue, he suddenly started caring for her.

'He got extremely drunk and told all my friends that he was in love with me and that I was his last chance at happiness,' she says. 'He then walked into the living room at a party in my sister's house, pulled a tuft out of his boxer shorts and set fire to his pubic hair in an attempt to get my attention.'

Jane first thought: 'Where's a real fire-truck when you need one?'

She decided to change her ways and stop playing games. She was not going to spend her life putting out the fire in another man's loins.

That night, she kissed her sister goodbye and walked out the door then and there, leaving John Player Blue's home-fires burning.

3

Sweet Sixty

For many people in their sixties, having grown up in harder times, raised children on a pittance and with punitive income tax and given everything they had to their offspring, their time has come. They have everything to look forward to. It's not all about free bus passes, you know.

Single or widowed, married or divorced, just because our grey or Grecian 2000-ed population is out of sight, it doesn't mean they are out of mind. We're not like Spain or Italy...or take your pick of any other European country where older people are revered and visible.

Older people here don't sit outside in parks playing backgammon. It's cold outside. The streets of our cities are dangerous. If they want to drive to their local pub in a rural area, they must drink Mi-Wadi when they get there. And stand outside in the street if they want to smoke a pipe.

Sometimes it's just easier to stay at home and watch *Fair City*.

Over-sixties are invisible. The streets of Dublin, Galway and Cork are filled with throngs of young kids on the rampage, like some post-apocalyptic Hollywood movie.

Advertisers aren't so interested because younger people have more disposable income. Television shows sell advertising too, so it's mostly young people who feature, unless there's some dumb joke about selling your granny. Even anti-ageist campaigns are accused of being ageist.

Over-sixties are having sex, looking up old boyfriends and girlfriends, reflecting on a life lived not in front of a computer screen but out on the land – they discovered organic food long before the trendy young things of Recession 2.0 did with their wicker baskets, clogs and farmer's markets – and carrying on when their one true love is no more.

They don't usually get included in books about sex and love and romance but they've probably had more of all the above than most younger people have had hot dinners. We cannot learn about ourselves without listening to those who went before us. We are who we are today because of them and the sacrifices they made. We carry their experiences around in our DNA. Sweet sixties? They rock.

TOGETHER AGAIN AFTER FIFTY YEARS #1

Sheila has a theory about marriage. 'The more attractive you are,' she says, 'the older you'll be before settling down.'

She believes the lookers want to spread their good fortune around. But there's a catch. She thinks they want to get jiggy only with other good-looking folk, which leaves those who are plain and homely on the shelves.

This might explain why she's only settling down now, moving in with Eddie, her childhood sweetheart, after being apart from him for more than fifty years.

They're not married but they say they are in love. They are like a pair of teenagers...again. They went to Yellowstone National Park, where they had summer jobs with students from all over America, working the soda fountain and selling postcards in return for the minimum wage and free accommodation.

Sheila lives in Monkstown and is a jovial Irish-American heading steady-as-she-goes into her seventies. She has short grey hair cut into soft curls and a plumpish, youthful vigour. As a star-spangled American, Eddie has a touch of the roly-poly vaudeville comic about him. He's a bald, diminutive firecracker.

It was 1952 when Sheila moved with her family to the US, to the idyllic town of New Haven, Connecticut. Sheila was sixteen and Eddie was twenty. In those days, the age difference was of little consequence. Sheila wore Eddie's high-school sweater and fraternity pin, a sign in the well-chaperoned, conservative world of post-war America that they were going steady.

Eddie recalls: 'A buddy of mine said, "Do me a favour. I'm going out with this girl and I need someone to double date." He told me she's nice-looking. She was very shy and pretty and innocent. All she was craving was a kiss goodnight.'

Sheila denies the 'craving' for modesty's sake but she did yearn for sex – or her idea of sex, a wanton feeling in the pit of her stomach. But when their song, Ray Noble's 'The Very Thought Of You', played on the radio, she thought about a life together: having their own apartment and pushing a pram up the high street.

At sixteen, that was her fantasy.

She says, 'Even today I remember that kiss on the cheek and it was so long ago. I don't know about you, Eddie, but I really was in love after that first kiss.'

'We'd been dating and it was my going-away party,' Eddie says. 'I was being stationed in Pennsylvania. I was standing on the veranda like an idiot and Sheila's girlfriend's mother pushed her out the door and she said, "Do your thing. Say goodbye."'

For the next sixteen months there was nothing but letter-writing. On a trip home, Eddie gave Sheila his high-school sweater and precious fraternity pin. 'From then on, we were going steady,' she says. 'I wasn't supposed to go out with anyone else. It's similar to doing a line but it's more official. It's showing off for the girl and a sense of possession for the guy. It's a pre-engagement but more flexible.'

It was flexible enough for Sheila to slowly begin dating other boys. 'I went to afternoon tea dances,' she recalls. 'I had a lot of men asking me out on dates, including a lot of Italian men who smelled of garlic. But,' Sheila whispers, 'you couldn't have sex.'

'You dreamt of it,' Eddie adds.

When Eddie went to serve in the Korean War, Sheila stayed at home to finish school and, as she remembers it, that was the beginning of the end of their relationship.

Eddie has a less romantic take on it. 'I came home from the Korean War one Christmas Eve, one-and-a-half years after we first met, and after a couple of months – she dumped me.

Four years later, Sheila realised she had made a mistake and got in touch with Eddie again when he was twenty-four and she was twenty. But by then, Eddie had already married.

'She blew it!' Eddie says today.

Eddie's older brother Jeff, who would play a vital role in their reunion fifty years later, was Sheila's biggest fan. He didn't like Eddie's second wife. He thought Eddie should have married Sheila.

Eddie didn't take his brother's advice about Sheila. He married twice and his first marriage lasted twenty-five years. 'Was I happy? I made the most of it. I was happy that I had three boys from that marriage. I was a buyer for a hydraulics company, a job I loved. For twenty years, I couldn't wait for my feet to hit the floor and to go to work.'

About twelve years ago, Eddie bumped into an old neighbourhood friend in New Haven and discovered that Sheila had moved back to Ireland and got divorced.

'I was told, "She lives in a mansion!" (It's a Victorian house in Monkstown.) The next time my brother called, I told him. Jeff said, "Well, what are you going to do about it?" I said, "I'm not going to do anything about it."'

And he wouldn't have either, had his brother Jeff not died. He died in Port Angel, East Washington...and left a bizarre bequest in his will.

Eddie flew out to take care of his affairs. Jeff used to collect ceramic jewellery boxes as a hobby. Eddie found one blue box, in which there was a ceramic egg. It said, "Love Me" on one side and had a note on the other saying, "For Sheila".

'From that moment on,' Eddie says, 'I was left with an albatross around my neck.' His brother, even in death, was playing Cupid. 'One day, I drove by Sheila's old college. I went in and was told she had been there for a reunion...three months earlier! So I wrote her a letter through the college: 'There is a bequest that Mr Jeff G. would like you to receive.' He signed the letter. And then he waited.

LOVING THAT MAN
'We lost our son, then my husband said he didn't love me.'

> Dear Q
> I was with my partner for twenty-two years, sixteen
> of them married. We loved each other dearly but
> we had our problems like everyone else. We also
> lost a son two months after he was born. Both
> my husband and I seemed to cope with our loss

and tried to get on with our lives as best we could, having two more sons. I noticed a big change in my husband shortly after losing our son. He had also got promoted and was working longer hours. I had a job and tried to make best for all us.

As the years passed, he slept a lot at home and did very little at all. Then he told me that he didn't love me any more and wanted a divorce. I was, of course, shocked as the night before he had told me he loved me and we had only moved into a new house three months before.

He refused to discuss any questions I asked as to why he had made his decision and two weeks later he left. Over the past two years or so, life has moved on. He lives in his own home. He recently told me that he has gone to counselling. I asked him why and he said, 'You know why.'

I have for a long time suspected that he was suffering from depression. Do I forget about him or try and get back together?

'Hoping'

Dear Hoping
You may eventually come to the realisation that you may always love him…in some way or other. But that doesn't necessarily mean that you can't look to the future with an open heart and allow yourself the possibility of falling in love again. For now you still don't have an answer to both your questions: why he wants a divorce and why he is seeking counselling.

It's a positive move that he has started counselling as it shows he's taking the initiative to sort his life out, clarify his feelings and deal with the grief/melancholia so he can better understand how he feels.

In time, he should have the answers you need and, ideally, be able to express them to you. It may help your relationship or not. He may love you but not wish to get back together. Or, as he said, he may not be in love with you any more but love you in a different way. You've given him both time and space.

Tell him gently, without pressure, that, in time, you would hope that he can provide clarity for both of you. Be his friend but prepare yourself emotionally for a new independent life. Start focusing on the other activities that would make you happy. Make time for yourself outside this relationship.

Your letter is about your husband and his happiness. And, although I know this directly relates to your future together, I also think it's important that – amidst all your concern for your husband – you do not forget about you.

THE HANDSOMEST MAN IN DONEGAL #1

Biddy is thinking about a question: what makes couples stay together through thick and thin? She's had her fair share of both. She sits in her bungalow in Falcarragh, Donegal, in her small living room, which is a year-round festival of doilies and family photographs. The question makes Biddy do something she does a lot of: giggle. What is the secret of a long and happy marriage?

'There's no secret,' says Biddy, who married her husband, known as Handsome Barney, in 1949.

'Ooh, aye. You take it one day at a time,' Biddy says. I wait for more. 'That's about all what's doing.' As they say in Donegal.

It's certainly easy to dismiss our parents' and grandparents' generations, where many marriages may have stayed afloat due to low expectations and high pulpits. But Biddy and Barney are different.

Even their names, Biddy and Barney, seemed right for each other. Their names have a zing. There had to be a sense of destiny.

Barney is known by family and friends as the handsomest man in Donegal. He and Biddy met at a dance in Dunfanaghy, which was even more isolated and poorer sixty years ago during the Second World War than the isolated place where they live now.

The handsomest man in Donegal? I had to see him. Even if he's the handsomest man in Falcarragh, he's now ninety-two. Biddy is a clean ten years younger.

Their little house overlooks the barren landscape, virtually unchanged for the last sixty years.

Biddy is rooting around in a sideboard in the living room of the bungalow she shares with Barney, a home immaculately kept. She's not going to bother with tea. She produces three glasses instead.

It's 3 pm. It's time not for tea but for a tipple.

Biddy has a nest of thick chestnut-brown curly hair, a full figure under her red pullover that must have kept men's hearts racing back in her youth, a pair of thick-rimmed glasses and a cheeky smile. Her arm is in a cast after a recent fall but she's not complaining. Unlike her husband, she is not the retiring type. It was she who spotted Barney at a local dance.

The first dance of the year was St Patrick's Day. 'You'd be waiting hard for that night to come,' Biddy says, 'and after that the next dance would be Easter Monday. You'd never have a dance on a Saturday night because you had Mass in the morning.'

While the dances were closely policed by clergy and adults (there was no alcohol), young people got properly acquainted afterwards.

The walk home along the lonely country lanes could take up to two hours but usually there was a posse of dance-goers, so they'd all set out and come home together on Friday nights, in the same way the community walked to Mass on Sundays. Unless, of course, a girl was fortunate enough to meet a boy, like when Biddy met Barney.

'A boy had to walk a girl home,' Biddy says. 'Then he'd have to walk to his home, which could be miles in the other direction. You were lucky if you met a boy with a bar on his bicycle.'

There were three people Biddy would be fearful of meeting on the road – day or night. A policeman. ('You'd be caught if you had no light on your bike.') A priest. ('I'd try and avoid them if I could.') And a doctor. ('They were apart from the rest of us. You'd never see a doctor's wife doing her own shopping. Not like today.')

She was less fearful of meeting cute boys. Which brings us back to Barney. Handsome Barney's absence, as he worked seasonally in Scotland, was the biggest factor in the first fifteen years of their marriage. The lack of jobs around these parts kept them apart summer after summer. Was Biddy not desperately lonely? Did she not cry herself to sleep at night? (I'm looking for TV movie-of-the-week emotion here: the tears, the drama, the goodbyes, the long days, the even longer nights and the passionate reunions.)

But Biddy's not biting. She's not evasive. She's just not into the Tears, Tantrums and Turnips School of Drama. There are no regrets, no recriminations, no anger at having been in a part of the country neglected by the powers-that-be in Dublin.

'I was working hard trying to keep the place going,' Biddy says. 'I was looking after the animals and getting the turf dried for the winter.' She pronounces it 'wunter', the way they do in Donegal.

Biddy may not have heard about cognitive therapy or the self-help books that clog the shelves in bookstores nowadays telling us how to improve our motivation or find love. But whether she realises it or not, she practises them beautifully.

She simply walks away from the negative thought. She pauses, thinks about it and keeps on giggling. 'I was too busy to be bored,' she adds. But she missed Barney? 'Oh, God, I did. I was counting the weeks until he'd be back. It seemed a very long time. He'd go away in the spring and wouldn't come back until about October.'

Biddy lets something slip. A clue. 'We had no time for fighting. I was too glad to see him coming back.'

There were no texts, no emails, no Skype, no web-cam and no Ryanair. We, who demand constant attention and devotion from out partners, forget that previous generations made do with prolonged periods of separation.

They didn't get bogged down in who said what to whom. Today's glossy tomes on relationships don't have chapters on what to do when your husband has to spend so much of the early years of your marriage abroad due to joblessness at home...

especially when this wasn't an unusual practice.

We hear footsteps and a rummage of pots. Barney is in the kitchen. (I suspect he's fixing his tie and dusting down his jacket.) The handle turns. The door slowly opens. This is it. The Handsomest Man in Donegal is finally here.

GOD'S GIFT TO WOMEN
'I'm in my sixties, separated, off the drink and have syphilis.'

Dear Q

I'm in my sixties. I've been sober for ten years after splitting with my first wife of thirty years. In my fifties, I took my freedom like a duck to water and contracted an STD, syphilis to be exact, which I thought was what young people get. I lived with a woman once in my life outside my marriage and she used to throw things at me, once leaving me with a cut above my eye. Younger women don't go for me, older single women tend not to be so interested in meeting someone of my age and, especially if they do want to and have had a hard time with the men in their life, they tend to tread very carefully. Do I have more to offer or am I fooling myself? I'm not exactly God's gift to women. But I'm not done yet.

'Left On The Shelf'

Dear Left

In some churches, I am sure you could cut the sexual tension with a hymn sheet. What about the personals? You get to pick the publication/website and market yourself wisely and they are nothing if not diverse. Plus, if a lonesome lady goes to the trouble of posting an ad, she's more likely to look benevolently on the male species.

But let's talk about you and your *nom-de-plume*. Left On The Shelf? You've dealt with and overcome enough in your life – alcoholism, domestic violence, syphilis, a broken marriage – to get a grip and realise that you're quite the catch. That's a lot of life experience you have there.

Stop feeling sorry for yourself. Rebuild your self-image and/or start writing your memoirs. That old adage, if you build it they will come, doesn't just apply to churches, art galleries and bookshops. Don't give up here. You will lure the right woman when you are your most confident self.

AFTER SHE'S GONE #1

His glasses slip down the end of his nose as he lifts himself up from his armchair to throw another peat briquette on the fire. He wheezes, tugs at his trousers, which sit just below his belly.

Harry lives in a former labourer's cottage in Greystones, County Wicklow. There are half-a-dozen other houses in a row, surrounded by hedges. The cottage has a back garden as large as a field (which still has an old, now unused outhouse). The bedroom is right off the sitting room and the galley kitchen looks out on to the hedgerow and gravel path in the tiny front yard.

It's not particularly cold outside but Harry's used to tending the fire. The house has no central heating. In fact, he only got electricity in 1956.

'When I got married there was no electricity and no flush toilets,' he says. 'We put our own toilets in with a septic tank.'

With the mass of trinkets, torn carpet and open fire, the house hasn't changed much in half a century. Harry is now in his late eighties and a nurse from the local health board pays him regular visits to make sure everything's ticking over.

He has been a widower for more than seven years and doesn't get out and about as much as he used to, although he'd be hard-pressed to give up the short walk to his local, where he enjoys a pint of stout with the other regulars, many of whom he's known since he was a blow-in from Dublin.

Harry recently turned down an invitation from his son – his only child – to watch a soccer match in England. Considering his age and the fact that they were to travel by ferry, I don't blame him.

His wife, Kay, died in 2000. She was four years older than him and smoked Sweet Afton for years until her doctor instructed her to give them up. In her youth, she loved a party. And in her latter years, she still liked a singsong.

Kay is everywhere. It is as if she had just popped into the kitchen to make a cup of tea. Although a rickety coffee table is decorated with a red PLO scarf. Since her death, Harry has obviously added his own touches.

Today, Harry doesn't look much different from the way he did in his sixties. There's a photograph of him and Kay on top of the television, attending a relative's wedding. It was taken about twenty years ago. He's bald, except for the odd strand of hair, with a broad build, round tortoiseshell glasses. He moves more slowly than he used to. 'I'm okay,' he says, not wanting anyone to feel sorry for him, 'aside from the old arthritis.'

Kay was always squished into her armchair: a small, rotund

woman with a soothing, crackly voice. It was not uncommon for her to have falls but she bounced back, usually with a bandage or two.

She always asked visitors to say a prayer for her. At her funeral, neighbours recall, Harry greeted guests, followed protocol and only once let his mask slip. As close friends and family lined up to kiss Kay goodbye, Harry stood stoically by until it was time to place the lid on her casket. He stepped forward, in a sudden burst of emotion. 'You were lovely, you were,' he said. 'You were lovely…'

At that moment, he seemed completely desolate without her.

Harry is a big, likeable man, originally from Sandymount.

He and his mate were on their way to a dance in 1947 when he met Kay and her friend standing at a bus stop. The band hadn't turned up. Had the band played, they probably would never have met. So they all went for drinks to the local pub… and she gave him the number of the house in Foxrock where she worked as a live-in housekeeper.

'My parish was in Sandymount,' Harry says, 'and Kay's was in Greystones but as she was working in Foxrock for more than five years, we had to get married there. A coal-porter getting married in a millionaire's parish.'

They got married on 8 September 1949 and had their reception in the Mount Hotel in Dún Laoghaire, which was paid for by the family Kay worked for. Then they went to Maynooth for their honeymoon.

Harry has a strong singing voice with a fine timbre. 'I used to sing,' he says. 'I sang at Labour Party meetings. I've been a member of the Labour Party all my life. I joined in 1945 and I'm still in it.'

94

'If I came home jarred of a Saturday night, I'd give Kay a lash of "Sweet Sixteen",' Harry says. It came in handy. 'I'd sing it so much, she'd be browned off with it.' Or maybe she'd just pretend to be. This was their song. He had sung it to Kay when she was a young lass, over and over again. Sometimes, she laughed and watched him give it his all; other times she just put up with the song when Harry was late home from work or had too many beers on board.

Or so she led him to believe.

He thought "Sweet Sixteen" drove her to distraction. It was only a lifetime later, when Kay fell ill, that he would discover just how much that song meant to her.

OLD JOB, NEW DAWN
'I'm sixty-two and I've been downsized! What to do?'

> Dear Q
>
> I've been working in an office-supply company as an administrator for ten years, essentially running the show and making sure everything is ticking over. The company has gone into receivership and is breaking up – as am I. I've been told I'm being downsized and, quite frankly, I don't know where to go from here. I'm sixty-two years of age and I'm not in a good position to start again with a new career or even continue with this one. This was just a job, it was only ever just okay but it was handy and reasonably well-paid.
>
> I live a contented life in my apartment in Wexford, have lots of friends, take a couple of charity adventure holidays every year – walking in

the Himalayas was one of the last – and, wisely I believe, don't exactly give the Irish male a five-star rating. (Been there, done that. I'm very happy to be single.) I'm free to do what I want but I don't honestly know what to do.

'Standing at the Crossroads'

Dear Standing

You seem to have settled into a steady, secure working routine and there's nothing wrong with that, except that it doesn't seem to have made you very happy.

You say that at sixty-two you're not in a good position to start afresh. On the contrary, with your life experience you're in a great position to do whatever you please.

What's this 'standing' business about? You just went walking in the Himalayas. I have no doubt you have a CV that will put all those twenty-, thirty-, forty-and fifty-something flighty young things to shame. You've been in this job for ten years.

Make a list of all the things you like to do with your time: reading, travelling, fundraising, organising, marketing. If you enjoy doing something you will inevitably be a success.

You don't have to make all these decisions right away. And you don't have to feel like you're typecast in the same career. You are your own casting agent. Also, there are many life coaches in Ireland who are trained in exactly this.

You could even rent out your flat for a year and travel the world. You will never meet a person who says, 'I've always regretted that time I travelled the world.' And rarely, if ever, will you meet someone who says, 'I have always regretted the time I left that job after ten years'.

You may not realise it now but your company has done you a great service (without meaning to, I might add). It has given you something better than stock options, a pay rise or a Christmas bonus. It has given you your freedom. Take it.

TOGETHER AGAIN AFTER FIFTY YEARS #2

Working as a tour guide in Dublin, Sheila was unaware that Eddie – her childhood sweetheart, the boy whose fraternity pin she wore with such pride, her first kiss, the man she hasn't seen in half a century since he went off to the Korean War – had been making enquiries about her on the other side of the Atlantic. Until, that is, his letter arrived.

Of course, she wasn't quite as rich as folks back in New Haven would have liked to believe. She wasn't living in a mansion but her house was large enough to allow her to rent out rooms to students and family friends.

Sheila married once and had three girls and two boys. When the marriage broke up she settled in Monkstown. Eddie had three boys from his first marriage; the second time he had married a much younger woman.

She had a comfortable life but when Eddie's letter finally arrived, the word 'bequest' caught her eye.

'I wasn't interested,' Sheila says. 'Then I thought about it for three weeks. A bequest for me? I looked up 'bequest' in the dictionary. It could have been a large sum of money or property! I always complained about being too poor so how could I turn my back on this?'

But she still wasn't convinced that calling Eddie after all these years would be worth it. She called and hung up. She thought again. Called again. Left a message. He phoned back and got Sheila's mobile number from the message on her answering machine.

When the call came through, Sheila was in Dunloe Castle in Killarney showing tourists around.

'My mobile phone rang as I walked through the bar, "The Very Thought of You" was playing on the piano,' she says. 'It was our song.'

Despite the coincidence, Sheila was no pushover. Nor was she a sentimentalist. Eddie knew that Sheila needed convincing, especially as her bequest was a ceramic – rather than a nest – egg. 'That was July 1999,' Eddie says. 'She sounded so interesting, so wonderful on the phone.'

'He did like the sound of my voice,' Sheila adds. 'I loved talking with him and I loved someone being so interested in me. But I didn't give him my address. It was great telling him the story of my life and I wanted it to continue. But I thought if he sent me the egg, it would all be over. And there was another reason…I also thought I should be cautious!'

Then Eddie said something he would never be able to take back. He told her he loved her.

'I had a friend in my kitchen,' Sheila says. 'I put my hand over the mouthpiece and told her, "He says he loves me!" Once he said that he loved me, I was hooked. Two months later I was due to go to my niece's wedding in America. I invited him to come.'

Eddie decided to pick up Sheila from Newark Airport in New Jersey in style. By now, he was working for a limousine transport company. Back in Ireland, word got out. 'My whole family – even my ex-husband – were really happy for me. So far, so good. But there was one thing left to do. They needed to exchange pictures…recent pictures.

Eddie had to come clean. He was not as slim as he used to be. 'If you ever saw his mother, she was huge,' Sheila says. 'I was concerned.'

'I sent her the picture first,' Eddie says.

'He was fat,' Sheila says, nudging Eddie before adding more onions to the frying pan. 'Tell him how much you weighed!

'I was 240 pounds,' Eddie says, finding it all terribly funny. 'But love is the best diet pill. I'm now 180.'

Sheila had better luck in the photograph stakes.

'She sent lots of goofy pictures. She absolutely looked dynamite! I thought, 'What am I going to do? I'm a big blob and she's a knock-out'!'

Eddie convinced his boss to allow him to use the Cadillac: 'At the airport, I saw this woman draped over a trolley with her granddaughter. No matter how many years go by, your eyes never change. I knew it was her right away. My heart was going…' Eddie pounds his chest with his fist. 'I kissed her on the cheek and felt her soft lips.'

Sheila's teenage granddaughter wasn't far off the age Sheila was when she first met Eddie. That makes it two lifetimes since they last met.

Off they went in the limousine – the lifestyle to which Sheila would have liked to become accustomed.

There was another problem. Eddie was all nerves. 'I've been in and out of Newark Airport a hundred and fifty times but I take off and I get lost. I hadn't a clue where I was. Sheila brought a CD of the Furey Brothers, which she put on the stereo.'

Sheila then did something which changed everything and set in motion Eddie's migration to Ireland. 'I had my hand on the gear stick,' Eddie says, 'and she put her hand on mine.'

They stopped at a Friendly's fast-food restaurant on the way back to Sheila's sister's house to have lunch. When Natasha, Sheila's granddaughter, went to the ladies' room, Sheila pulled Eddie's collar toward her and – as Eddie says – 'puckered her lips'.

Natasha was back just in time to see their first kiss in fifty-two years. 'Natasha comes out and sees granny smooching, right there in Friendly's!' Sheila says. 'I had in my mind to get him into the bushes and make love to him, I was so starved.'

She was no longer the demure girl he once knew. When they got back to Sheila's sister's house, Eddie carried the bags to Sheila's room. At sixty-seven, she was no longer the shy teenager she once was. But, as Eddie testifies, she still had it: 'When the door was closed she was on me like a blanket!'

After the wedding reception ended at about 1.30 am, they rented a room in a 'low-grade motel'. They got home at 7 am. Sheila's brother-in-law was out jogging and spotted them smooching on the path.

He started calling her Aunty Mame.

There was one little problem. Eddie was still married to his second wife of twelve years, who was fifteen years younger than him.

'They're divorced now,' Sheila says.

'And she got lots of money,' Eddie adds.

'Eddie's got a huge heart,' Sheila says.

When Eddie visited Sheila several months after their tryst

at the wedding, her feet were back on the ground. 'I felt I had to let him come,' she says. 'I felt I owed him hospitality. But I was quite prepared that it wouldn't work out.' She took him around the west of Ireland and they stayed at Bunratty Castle. 'He got Limerick as a bonus.'

After a time, Eddie gave Sheila a diamond ring. 'Love doesn't die,' he says. 'There's no number on it. We first met in 1952 and we got back together after a lifetime apart in 1999. Maybe everything that happened in between was necessary.'

TWO DRESS SIZES, TWO DECADES LATER
'I have struggled with my weight for twenty years!'

Dear Q

I am about two stone overweight. That mightn't be much to some people but I am only five feet tall. I used to be size ten and, since giving up smoking nearly two years ago on my doctor's orders, I have gone up two dress sizes. I have tried dieting but it just puts me in a bad mood as I have always eaten what I like. I eat healthily but I do like my chocolate as well.

I joined a gym a couple of months ago and, due to work commitments, didn't get there as often as I would like but I have since started going regularly for the past two weeks. But when I don't start seeing results straight away I just start thinking, 'What's the point?'

When I was in my forties, I was too busy being a wife and mother to worry about it. I always said I couldn't live with myself at the weight I was then but I did. In my fifties, I piled the weight on.

I think I am pretty and I like myself. But lately I don't even want to buy clothes. I think I would carry it better if I was taller but that isn't going to happen now. My daughter has brought up my weight in arguments and, while I know she didn't mean it, that has stayed with me. Growing up, my sister did the same. I am now past middle age and the spread just keeps spreading. Do you have any suggestions?

'Feeling Fat'

Dear Feeling

Dress size appears to have been a weapon of mass destruction your family used against each other. You have learnt to define yourself and others by the amount of space you take up in the world.

Some families/people use college grades, careers, money, designer clothes and IQ to see how they measure up to one another and the world.

You are so much more than a dress size (or two). How do you free yourself? Acknowledge that you are playing the game, that you are a willing pawn in this charade.

Perhaps you have little else going on for yourself at the moment. Or perhaps a little part of you – the inner critic that keeps you amused, busy or flagellating yourself – enjoys it.

You shouldn't need one quality that makes you feel better or worse about yourself. The world is too big. Life is too short. This is not just about two dress sizes. This is about your attitude to yourself and to others, and your ability to start afresh and leave the scars of the past behind you, even if you decide to leave your size ten dresses behind also.

Don't listen to that inner critic. But I guess you already knew that.

THE HANDSOMEST MAN IN DONEGAL #2

The kitchen door opens. In walks a man with skin that is creamy, soft and remarkably unlined. He still has a respectable head of silver hair, two rosy cheeks that don't show any sign of giving up their youthful vigour any time soon and a boyish modesty and palpable shyness.

Barney shakes my hand. He has big, soft hands. This from a man who spent most of his working life as a farm labourer? He's grinning ear to ear. He's in a green tweed suit, with a matching shirt and bottle-green jumper underneath, wearing a reliable wristwatch with a round gold face and black strap. He has been expecting company.

They don't do style like this any more. Despite the drumroll in my head as I watched the handle on the kitchen door turn, there's nothing flashy about him.

We have a glass of Biddy's homemade tipple. It warms us all up, which you would need in the wilds of Donegal, with an unrelenting wind rattling the gutter outside.

But back to that dance in Dunfanaghy, Barney asked to see Biddy home. 'And,' Biddy says, 'that was the beginning of it.' Then Barney went to Scotland to work on a farm every summer until 1964. 'Didn't you come back in the winter, Barney?'

'Oh, aye,' Barney says. 'I went to Scotland first in 1945, the year the war ended.' He's off. He appears shy at first but he's a talker!

'I worked from 8 am to 5.30 pm every day in Roxburghshire. Then I got an offer of a job on the Isle of Arran. I packed me wee case. I didn't want to pass the boss's house. I walked down a laneway a mile or so to get to the station. Aye! Do you know the first food I ate on the Isle of Arran? A feed of porridge. That's what they had for dinner. I changed my clothes and went out to the field to work.'

The same day?

'Aye, turning turnips. Nine pence for 200 yards. The other men were on their knees. I asked for a hoe.'

Turning turnips?

Biddy interrupts: 'They were growing like wee shamrocks and you had to transplant them. But, Barney, that's nothing to do with us…'

Barney's not giving up that easily. 'I'd come back home and would be away back in the spring again of the next year, then…'

'And anyway, we got married in January 1949,' Biddy interjects again, drawing a line under his turnips with an imaginary hoe.

Biddy wants to swerve Barney away from the turnips to the pulpit and their wedding day.

The ceremony took place at eight in the morning, she says. 'There was no fuss or bother about getting married. You'd cycle to the church and let the priest know. There were no white dresses or veils. People couldn't afford them.'

Mostly, newlyweds got married in the morning and had a party back at their house to dance through the night and – Biddy says – with 'a couple of chickens boiled on the stove'. But Biddy and Barney didn't do that. Instead, they honeymooned in Derry. 'Oh, aye! We were right toffs,' Biddy laughs.

However, no sooner were they hitched then Barney had to

go back to Scotland to toil on the land. And so it continued.

They had two girls and one boy, and now have three grandchildren. Their girls live in Dunfanaghy: one owns a shop, the other works part-time after the factory she worked in closed down. Their son works as a 'chippie' in London, as a carpenter doing loft conversions. When he was born in 1964, Barney decided to find work at home. They grew potatoes, hay and corn and also kept a few pigs.

But when Ireland entered the Common Market, both the pigs and the feed became too expensive.

When Barney did come home, he joined the other men for games of cards late into the night, while Biddy stayed at home with her three kids, knitting socks and gazing at the stars. Still, she'd always wait up for Barney to come home, even if it was 2 am or later. Barney would sometimes play for geese and ducks.

'And the women were left home watching the winds,' Biddy adds. Barney grins guiltily, his cheeks glowing.

Biddy does have a theory on why marriages lasted longer back then. 'They all have too much money now and are having too good a time of it. When women have a baby they've nothing to do but throw their babies in the car and go here and there. When we had babies, we had to sit in and look after them. When we had a row, there was no pulling out anywhere. We had no money or car. Everybody stuck at it then whether you were happy or not. It was for life. Now it's until you meet the next one you fancy!'

Of course, Biddy and Barney rowed. Big ones. When they did, they wouldn't speak for a day and then they'd get over it. There was no gentleman's club, no sleeping on the couch, nowhere to run away to even if they wanted to.

It's getting late. The sky is full of gloomy clouds. The fields beyond their house are turning from green to a hazy blue. Not much changed from the way they were fifty, maybe a hundred years ago. The roads are better but there's little new housing around here.

'The night is closing in already,' Biddy says. 'It used to be clear until eleven or twelve o'clock and now it's starting to get dark at nine. We didn't get much sunshine this year. But we'll have to carry on.'

They've made it this far. Any regrets?

'Oh,' Biddy adds, 'I don't think we'll bother getting divorced now.'

Then Handsome Barney looks across the room at his wife and, like a big teenager, he blushes.

ME, MY HUSBAND AND I
'I think I want out of my crisis-stricken marriage.'

Hi Q

I've recently hit the big six-o. I've been married for twenty years, most of which time has been plagued by financial worries, arguments, too much TV, bad food, one cancer scare, a near-fatal accident with one of my two children (which took her six months to recover from) and good old-fashioned boredom. We usually speak through the children to make our point or simply talk about the children…nothing else. Our sex life has long since vanished. Part of me loves my husband and part of me dislikes what he/we have become. I want out. At least, I think I want out.

I'm reaching a crossroads. I'm fearful of another

twenty years of the same – and I don't know what to do.

'Stuck in a Twenty-Year Limbo'

Dear Stuck

You've both struggled to stay afloat and stay sane for twenty years. Through all your troubles, you've managed to keep the technicalities of your marriage together but you're just going through the motions. Life is too short. The first thing you need to do is sit your husband down, prepare for a marathon discussion and tell him what you told me. Cry. Cry until it hurts and keep talking. Get it out. Don't let it fester any more. Tell him you love him but you're cracking up under the burden.

The frank exchange of views – although long overdue – should open up a new era of openness and be shocking for you both. It's nothing that can be glossed over. Ask him if he's happy. Tell him you're not. But tell him why.

AFTER SHE'S GONE #2

The rota of chores keeps Harry occupied. As a slip of a man, he delivered coal to the flats of Dublin's Townsend Street at Christmas during Alfie Byrne's tenure as Lord Mayor of Dublin. Byrne endeared himself to the working classes with gestures like carrying sweets in his pocket for the street urchins of Dublin and authorising the Christmas coal-runs.

'We carried ten-stone bags of coal,' Harry says, 'not the eight stone bags of today. We went to the top of every flat in Dublin. They'd come out and say, "Is that the Mansion House coal?" And we'd pour it into the tea chests on the landing.'

After landing a job at Wallace's Coal Merchants in Ringsend, he walked from his little house to Greystones, rising at 4.30 to catch the 7 o'clock bus, which brought him to Westland Row at 7.45. Locals got to know this former Dubliner on the roads and gave him lifts, which was rare as there were few cars around. 'It felt a damp climate on those mornings, I can tell you.'

He never grows tired of talking about his son, Tomás. Tomás is aware of this, judging by the souvenir plates covering the walls from all over the world: Romania, Hollywood, Bulgaria, Argentina. And there are the spooky dolls in their national dress in a glass cabinet in the corner. Tomás brings his dad back these mementos from international rugby and soccer matches.

The phone rings once and then stops. It rings a second time. 'He always rings twice,' Harry says, after exchanging a few words. 'There was a man up the road who was calling me every day, as late as ten o'clock at night. He got very bossy. He wanted to take over my life. Tomás always gives it a ring first, so I know it's him.'

Tomás was born in 1954 after a rocky pregnancy. Kay had already suffered one miscarriage and she was rushed to Holles Street Hospital seven months into her pregnancy. 'The doctor said, "This is serious, the baby is crossed in your missus. We'll have to operate." They took her to Meath Street from Holles Street.'

Harry's voice falters. 'I get a bit overcome, you know? When I got to the hospital, he was nine hours old. He was blue, like a fish. The doctor said he had a murmur in his heart but it would go if he made it to ten years.' And he did. 'One year became two, then he was three, four, five…'

'Tomás wasn't raised here, he was raised next door,' he says.

Were space and money tight? 'They just took a fancy to him. They said leave him here for the night. That became the week and it went on from there…We cut an arch in the hedge between the gardens and he'd come and go.' A brother and sister, cousins of the family, lived next door.

At fifteen, Tomás left school and got a job in a nearby industrial estate, as a cutter in a shirt factory.

Harry's eyes redden, two whirlpools of tears. It is Tomás who keeps him in such independent, cheerful spirits. He's not here every week. But Harry is consoled all the time just by his existence.

There are dates Harry quotes: 8 September 1949 (his wedding day); 28 February 1954 (the day of Tomás's birth) and, most proudly, 18 October 1974, the day Tomás started working in the civil service, where he remains to this day.

A local TD told Harry, 'You'll kill yourself with that coal,' and offered him a job as a cleaner at Leinster House. Harry had a better idea: he bought a ladder and worked as a window cleaner. 'I stuck it until I was seventy, until I couldn't get up the ladder any more.'

The job at Leinster House he passed onto his son: on 18 October 1974. 'I said, "Would you do it?" He said, "I would, Dad!" He started that day, cleaning the toilets and the brasses in the ministers' offices.'

'I couldn't have married a better woman,' he says. 'She had a heart of gold.'

If I got drunk and came home at one in the morning, she'd never breathe a word. 'Well, I sang that song.' What song? '"Sweet Sixteen". It's the only song she complained about.'

He could have had fewer jars a little less often, he says. 'But I never left her short of wages. Every Friday I'd have her few bob and lay it on the table and she'd appreciate that as much as if it were a million pounds. That I did, that I did.'

'She'd be sitting right there without a cross word,' he says, pointing at her empty armchair, 'banging away on her rosary.'

Harry is a man who wanted enough space to do his thing. Today he maintains that freedom. Even during their marriage, it was her gift to him. She's gone. He's alone. And, as he sees it, that's that.

On her deathbed, Kay put in an unusual request. 'Harry,' she asked him, 'sing me "Sweet Sixteen".'

Yes, that song again, even though she sometimes protested when he sang it during their marriage.

This time he sang it to her in her final hours, not to pacify or entertain her but as a celebration. And this time she loved it.

Before I leave Harry to make his dinner, I ask him to give me a few bars of "Sweet Sixteen". He takes a big, hefty breath:

> *Last night I dreamt I held your hand in mine*
> *And once again you were my happy bride*
> *I kissed you as I did in Auld Lang Syne*
> *As to the church we wandered side by side*

He can't remember all the lyrics now. But he keeps trying. 'As to the church we wandered side by side…' I imagine Kay out there somewhere, silently mouthing the lyrics as her husband struggles with the chorus, helping him to find the words.

4

At Rainbow's End

Heard the one about the young gay guy in a bar who was asked what age he was when he came out? 'Out?' he said. 'Darling, I was never in.' That conversation happened not so long ago in the Dragon bar in Dublin. It's hard to believe that the coming-out rite of passage may soon be no more. Irishmen are more willing to be openly gay. Lesbians are also more visible, setting up camp in the Front Lounge in Dublin on Friday nights. They too have experienced a mini-renaissance in gay culture.

The Front Lounge is probably one of the few bars in Ireland where men and women have no romantic interest in each other: it's the men on one side of the bar, and the women on the other, like a céilí, without the nuns and priests. There is no need to measure the distance between the sexes with a ruler.

A tall, busty, blonde woman in the Fitzwilliam Hotel wears a T-shirt with the slogan, 'We Have Come for Your Wives.' The visibility of gay women is fast catching up with that of their male counterparts.

But take a guy who is now thirty. He would have seen both worlds: the old and the new. He would likely have arrived on the scene in his late teens or early twenties before the new generation of drag queens and gay TV presenters.

Dublin still lacks a gay theme-park or quarter, like Soho in

London, but it's certainly got the gay old merry-go-round along Lower George's, Parliament and South William Streets.

In 'Jurassic Park', the gay bar-room in the George on Dublin's South Great George's Street, where the older gay men hang out, the patrons share a history. Some of them might have been married. Some may still be married.

They know what this country was like before decriminalisation in 1993. Many took part in gay pride marches before it was fashionable, before little old ladies in plastic headscarves stood at bus stops and blew kisses at the gay boys and their colourful floats as they rolled by. Some still fight the fight. Others have settled down, with children, and passed the baton.

Ireland's Queer Archive, only recently introduced into the National Library after decades in a lock-up on the Kylemore Road, chronicles thousands of forgotten, battered batons among its quarter-of-a-million press clippings and over three hundred world magazines going back to 1951. In them, there are many thrilling advertisements for nightclubs of yore: Mildred at Da Club, Disco Outcomers in Drogheda, Shaft, Hurray Henry's at the Powerscourt Townhouse Centre, Oscar's at the Olympia, Powderbubble at Red Box, Ham at the Pod. They promised the earth; they were where many love stories began.

THE GAZELLE, THE WOLF AND THE EXOTIC BIRD #1
Michael and Robert are sitting in the George with two pints in front of them, bouncing along excitedly to the music. They're twitching like two gazelles who are wary that the odd lone wolf might take the seat opposite them or, if they're lucky, half-a-dozen more playful gazelles could come galloping in the door any moment.

Thumping dance music from Ireland's cruisiest gay bar

can be heard on the approach from several blocks away. It was unrivalled until the Dragon opened, also on George's Street, an oriental themed mega-bar that – for the first time in gay Dublin's history – holds up well against any of Ireland's snazziest straight bars, a reputation that was consolidated when opera singer Cara O'Sullivan one night silenced the heaving mass in the upstairs beer garden by singing a few notes.

But the George has its place. It has now become a wry allusion to its seedier past. Through the windows blurry figures mingle, slouch against the glass, drinking beer, waiting for their tall dark strangers. They'd be hard-pressed to find them here. It celebrates its meat-market vibe, with its purple décor and gold cherub statuettes, but it's a post-modern meat market. This is the kind of bar that wouldn't have looked out of place in London's Soho in the 1960s

It's 11 o'clock on a Thursday night. We are in the midst of what's known in gay parlance as 'the scene'. Michael, twenty-nine, and Robert, twenty-one, are mad into sports: the former karate, the latter GAA.

Michael is short and stocky, with brown hair and a laddish smile. He laughs a lot and, wearing a pair of blue jeans and a bomber jacket, he looks like a sporty jock or a dishevelled former boy-band member, who has packed on a couple of extra pounds. He is studying sociology.

His boyfriend Robert takes quick, manic sips of his pint: one more and he'll be up on the dance-floor. Robert is noticeably shyer than Michael. But that won't last. Michael calls Robert 'pup,' with affection.

Robert is slim with broad shoulders, the result of his regular GAA workouts. He works for a multinational computer company, the kind that's big enough to have gay and lesbian social groups like the Gay Googlers, otherwise known as the Gayglers.

They're both new economy kids, from their chinos to their buoyant bank accounts and the rolls of €50 notes in their back pockets.

One-and-a-half pints later, the disco has started. Robert has been itching to get up on that dance floor. Off he goes, doing a pretty good Justin Timberlake impression, swinging his hips and moving his forearms back and forth as if he's lifting weights.

Michael's first love was a girl. He was in his teens, growing up in a cosy three-up, three-down in Drogheda with his parents and two brothers. She wasn't the girl next door but she was close.

'She lived around the corner,' he says. 'I never thought of boys romantically. Except for one guy at school who I fooled around with from fourteen to seventeen, there was no real romantic attachment.'

'We started looking at porn, messing around at home and then we'd go back outside to hang out with our girlfriends.'

'At school, nobody would have called me a faggot because I would have beaten the shit out of them,' he adds.

Michael has been a stalwart of the scene for over ten years, excluding his wilderness year in Sydney, Australia when he left college. He hit the gay scene in the early 1990s when gayness was still invisible on the Irish main street.

'In Drogheda, circa 1988,' Michael says, 'there were no role models.' His gay neighbours were invisible. Gay couples, wherever they were, didn't move to suburbia and live in a three-bedroomed semi-d and save for a kitchen extension. It was too bleak and homogenous a place for that.

But there was one visibly gay man. He was rake-thin, over six feet, had prematurely grey hair, an equally pale complexion and wore colourful flared trousers.

He was wildly, instinctively, Mosney Holiday Camp flamboyant: he swayed when he walked, leant slightly on one leg when he stood in line at the local chipper. He peered over his shoulder in a coy, cautious manner when – as would happen frequently – local kids would roar names at him and then run for their lives. 'If he sat on the top of the double-decker bus along with the rest of the mortals,' Michael recalls, 'the lads would nudge each other.'

He was a taller, more shabbily dressed version of one of the characters from *Are You Being Served?* But he wasn't trying to be – not in this lower-middle-class suburb where there wasn't even a main street – he was merely being himself.

He sounds like an undernourished exotic bird from a warmer climate who lost his way and found himself drained of all colour, stranded in that cold, grey, concrete town.

'When I saw him I'd get a sinking feeling in my stomach,' Michael says. 'There was no glamour about him whatsoever. He mostly kept to himself.'

He was out of context, even when he went to the church on Sundays, when it was a community event and packed to the rafters. 'I was surprised to see him taking his place in the pew alongside everyone else,' Michael adds.

Why? Because, among the allegedly solid family units and screaming babies he seemed to be an outsider? Because, knowing that this was a small community in a small, insular country with a large church-going public, he should have been above this ritual? Because Catholicism condemned homosexuality and here was an openly gay man receiving Communion?

Because he was too extraordinary for any of it?

'All the above,' Michael says.

Michael did, however, find out one piece of information about him that changed everything. He found out his name. It was an ordinary name. It made him less exotic.

The man, I suggest, lived his life free from the expectations and disapproval of others as he stood in the chipper with his flared trousers and his coquettish, Princess Diana half-smile. Perhaps there *was* a role model who had enough self-belief to put on his well-worn and sometimes too-short flared trousers and be himself.

'I never thought of it like that,' Michael says. 'Nice one.'

Robert is waving from the dance floor. He doesn't want to stop but he doesn't want to keep dancing on his own like a Nobby-No-Friends.

'Come on,' Michael says. 'It's "I Will Survive". Again. We must do this more often.' But I don't see him again properly for another six weeks. The Michael I meet then is more world-weary than the Michael working up a sweat on the dance floor tonight. But none of us know what's around the corner, so for now with big grins and laughter drowned out by the music, we are happy to keep on dancing.

WALLED IN
'I'm gay and terrified to let people get to know me.'

Dear Q

I have developed a well-honed mechanism of self-protection over the last few years, mainly because I'm gay and I always had this secret that I had to withhold from people. When I was still coming to terms with my sexuality, I had my front to ward people off. As I have grown more comfortable with my homosexuality, I am still preventing others from getting through the barrier. I alienate and avoid people, even ones I quite like, because, deep down, I fear that if they really got to know me, the real me, they would reject me.

I had my first real gay relationship last winter. It ended because I wanted it to but all the time throughout it, my boyfriend kept saying that I was too distant, that I wouldn't let him get to know me. I spoke to a counsellor afterwards and she said that I have a massive inferiority complex and low self-esteem. She came to this conclusion after a conversation with me in which I told her about how I always felt different from my family because I had very little in common with my siblings and that I was always made to feel different, even if my family didn't intentionally set out to do that.

I always thought that I was just being hypersensitive. My father is also a long-time alcoholic: not a severe or abusive one but one with an alcohol problem that is conducted 'in secret' and was never discussed or acknowledged, even though we all knew what was going on. My dad is a lovely man who would do anything for us (except stop drinking which he can't or won't) but I always believed that the secrecy surrounding his problem couldn't be good for our family or for us as his children.

I'm just finishing college and over the last few months I've got to meet a lot of new people, either through others or through a new job that I have started. Some of these people are gay and really nice and I would like to keep in touch with them because I don't have many gay friends, not in Dublin where I live and work.

But I find myself falling back into the same habit: I don't text or call because it involves me reaching out to them. I'm afraid that they won't like me, so I'm thinking that it can't be about fear of rejection due to my sexuality, not any more. I find that this is affecting my sex life too: I've met a few guys over the last few months, and each time, I was so nervous about how I was 'performing' (for want of a better phrase) that I just couldn't enjoy it. Come to think of it, I don't honestly think I've ever really enjoyed sex, not the way that I feel I should and the way others do. That makes me so depressed that I could just cry.

I'm a shy person but not cripplingly so. I have my small band of close friends with whom I am popular but the ones I'm really close to live in my hometown. I'm warm, funny, charming, intelligent, a good conversationalist – once you get to know me. And that's where I need some help. I just can't let people in. I'm entering a new phase in my life that I'm really excited about. I just don't want to spend any more Saturday nights on my own: I've done it for long enough already. Thanks for listening.

'Feeling Different'

Dear Different

We all have friendships in life that last five months, five years, five days, five minutes, or sometimes a lifetime. Good or bad, short or long, they leave us a little richer (or smarter). They start on a wing and a prayer and sometimes they end through no fault of their own: because it's tough to find people in this world with whom we're compatible, in an intimately social way: people we can divulge our greatest fears to, our finest ambitions, our deepest insecurities…the best of ourselves and, yes, the worst of ourselves. The latter, of course, is all a matter of interpretation.

What I see as among the best in you is being gay, coming to terms with it, finding your feet in a relationship and knowing that you still have a way to go on that journey of self-discovery – to feeling so comfortable with yourself that sex becomes more enjoyable.

While you don't appear to believe that being gay is the worst of yourself, you don't yet appear to rate it highly enough. This doesn't mean you need to go on a Gay Pride march but it does mean that you will at some point celebrate it privately and say to yourself, 'I wouldn't swap me for all the tea in China.'

This brings me to the next part of your letter: taking that leap of faith, calling others, inviting them to your home, arranging friendship dates. Friendships commonly blossom through a shared interest. ('You like X, Y, Z? Me too!') But that shared interest is usually a way of swapping numbers, arranging that first, tentative friendship date, where you are both like schoolkids again, eager to impress each other and share some of your beliefs.

Growing up in a home where there are secrets, such as a father's alcoholism, can also steel you against the world. If you feel compromised, if you feel that it stops you being you, listen to that. Just like dealing with your homosexuality, dealing with a family secret can mess with your head, giving you the 24/7 notion that you have something to hide, that you are different, apart from others.

I can't help thinking that insecurity and low self-esteem are a short-cut explanation for a lot of things. We're all self-conscious, awkward, shy kids in the playground from time to time. We all have barriers of some form or other, yours are a little higher, maybe. Sometimes, we give prospective friends (and ourselves) a chance by choosing to ignore them.

Whether it's revealing your father's alcoholism or celebrating your gayness (privately or otherwise), at some point you will find that you will be too preoccupied by the complexities, mysteries and beauty in others to think about what you bring to the equation.

With time, the right guy and some self-examination in a controlled environment, you will find great sex and true friends.

DREAMING OF HAPPY EVER AFTER #1

In a Lucan semi-d, with an open of bottle of wine on the table, Martha is sitting down to dinner with Aran, her twenty-one-year-old son, and his stepfather, Simon. Martha's seventy-year-old mother lives in the back garden in a small, purpose-built house. She waves from the garden.

Aran is a tall, mature, well-behaved kid, who never had a girlfriend, although plenty of female friends, and has just finished studying travel and tourism. He wears false tan. He is centred, unusually so for someone of his years. 'He was like that when he was three years old,' Martha says. 'He was exactly the same.'

Simon and Martha are veteran clubbers who have just hit forty.

Growing up, Aran's best friend from primary school was a guy who once dressed up as Cher for a fancy-dress party and carried it off with aplomb. That was a big clue. It wouldn't take Perry Mason to figure out that Martha's son was gay. Simon saw Aran through clear eyes: he figured out long ago that he was gay but knew he had to wait until Aran was ready to tell Martha.

In fact, Aran's two best school friends were gay: one a girl, the other a boy. He was already in good hands. He has a maturity and self-respect that belong to a country where homosexuality was legalised only fifteen years ago, where boys who like boys walk down the street hand-in-hand (rarely, granted), where there are fledgling programmes to deal with homophobic bullying in schools and where gay teenagers have each other, oblivious to the constraints of the early 1990s, when they were just toddlers.

Sitting at the dinner table with his green T-shirt, trimmed

in sunflower yellow, short spiky hair, long, slim arms and quasi-rebellious arrow-piercing in his chin, Aran's self-assurance is also consolidated by his parents' relationship. It's taken them a long time and several previous partners to get here.

This is an ordinary family with ordinary problems. What's less ordinary is that – for the most part – they all get along. They slag each other off. They argue a little. But if all families are dysfunctional to some degree, this is a functional dysfunctional blended family.

Aran has tips for those younger than him. This time regarding his tan. It does look natural. Has he been away? 'Tanning wipes from Penneys,' he says. 'You run them across your face like this.' He demonstrates with his napkin. Simon eats his chili con carne. Martha muffles a smile at the mention of the wipes. She's not crazy about them.

Some people forget that for young gay men, who have grown up in a predominantly heterosexual world, the gay scene can be uncomfortable and scary. 'When you're new to the scene, it can be intimidating, and some men might try to exploit that,' Aran says. 'But it is becoming more easygoing, even over the last couple of years.'

Aran missed much of the gay rights' campaign. Young men don't need older men like they used to. They have friends their own ages. Aran kisses cute boys. But his main priority is not sex, it's a healthy and stable relationship.

At Simon's fortieth birthday in Ron Black's in Dublin's Dawson Street, as Aran got up to leave at the end of the evening, Simon gave Aran a paternal kiss on the cheek and asked him when he'd be home. That night, true to form, Martha also got a rundown on Aran's plans for the night: 'What time will you be home? Do you have enough money?' And the old mantra that has served them both well, 'Stick with your pals.'

Simon, Martha and Aran are just so bloody, refreshingly ordinary. In a wider context of cultural change in Ireland over the fifteen years since the decriminalisation of homosexuality, that's some kind of achievement.

It's their lack of issues that makes them an issue. The irrelevance of Aran's sexuality, of Simon and Martha's new relationship, of Aran's father in Canada, makes them relevant.

Simon and Martha both had contentious relationships with their own fathers: Simon's was authoritarian; Martha's was an alcoholic. However, they've broken the chain.

Simon's parents were old-school, or as he puts it, 'repressed'. His late father once found a packet of condoms in his son's drawer. He brandished them and demanded, 'What is *this*?' Simon, a smart-ass, told his father, 'Well, if you don't know now, you'll never know.' When he left school, his father wanted him to study finance or some other stable profession. But he moved to London and got a job in a bookie's and rang his father to tell him. 'I got a job as an accountant,' he shouted down the phone, 'a fucking turf accountant!'

Martha and Simon moved in together in 2003 after Martha's ten-year marriage broke down.

Simon, coincidentally, lived just around the corner with his then girlfriend. When Simon sold his old house, he bought Martha's ex-husband out of the house and they completely refurbished it. 'Not even a plug fitting remains,' Simon says.

Martha realises that each nuclear family has its own kitchen-sink dramas. Despite the fact that her alcoholic father became rowdy from time to time, nothing is ever as it seems. She grew up in a cul-de-sac in Athlone and her mother would be ashamed to face the neighbours after her father began drinking.

One fine day, Martha told her mother, 'Number Two live in abject poverty. Number Three's husband is having an affair. Number Four's father is a fucking thug. Number Five, Six, Seven, Eight and Nine are normal. But Number Ten has crazy, out-of-control kids.'

Martha and Simon took the lessons from the past and, with Aran, created a blended family of equals. They weren't always so open with each other but one night it happened…

Five years ago, Aran called Martha from town and told his mother he needed to meet her urgently. She was in a heap. Simon knew. This was it; this was Aran's coming out. Martha suspected that he had got a girl pregnant. As she rushed out the door to meet her son, she wondered, 'What the hell is going on?'

UNDER THEIR ROOF
'My boyfriend won't stand up to his parents about being gay!'

Hi Q

I'm gay and I'm seeing an eighteen-year-old guy who's doing his Leaving Cert. We have loads in common, get on well and frequently discuss our future together. We often admit to being in love and I have no reason to think we're not. We live far apart and only see each other on weekends, which is frustrating but just bearable. It's his first relationship and his parents have just realised that he is gay – although they and he refuse to talk about it.

They have asked that I never contact them again and have forbidden him from seeing me.

His parents are total rednecks with no social

graces whatsoever and they are very, very strict with their son. Now, I don't want him to leave home – although he was willing to do that for me – as his Leaving Cert is the first priority. I simply want him to tell his parents that he intends to keep seeing me as he is an adult and should have the right to choose his own friends. He has turned into a complete sheep and keeps suggesting he's going to say something but ultimately never does. He's too frightened of his parents.

I know he's young and I can't and shouldn't encourage him to do something that would be against his best interests. But it upsets me that he's not willing to make any sort of stand.

He knows that I miss him and that I resent having to wait months. In other words, how long do I wait? What can I say to him without having to give him an ultimatum? I do love him, before you ask, but his spineless tendencies lately have been very off-putting. He seems happy to keep his parents content and me upset. Am I being unfair to him or vice-versa?

'Lost in Leitrim'

Dear Lost

I don't believe that thinking of his parents as 'rednecks' helps your case one way or another, regardless of their social skills. And, whether or not you stood up to your parents at eighteen or older, your boyfriend is on his own trajectory. He's feeling enough pressure, I'm sure, as it is, with his impending exams, his parents looking at him differently and, of course, his boyfriend whom he has been forbidden to see.

Yes, he's an adult. Yes, he's eighteen. But he is financially dependent on his parents and living under their roof, while he is studying for his exams at least. And that's not even taking into account the emotional trauma he must feel, not being able to get support from the two people who raised him. Regardless of the history – you may have set up the local gay and lesbian branch in your town, for all I know – your boyfriend does not deserve your resentment.

In this context, I find it difficult to see your boyfriend as spineless. It's easy for anyone (me included) to sit objectively on the outside and make judgement calls. Even at eighteen, most people have an awful lot of soul-searching and growing up to do, and life experiences ahead of them that will shape the people they will eventually become. You are obviously at different stages in your lives. Perhaps, this is not the right time to take the relationship further.

WHEN OPPOSITES ATTRACT #1

When they attended a recent pub quiz, Jennifer and Ciara called themselves the Venn Diaphragms. It was a lesbian pub quiz in aid of charity so it was an all-female joke, one that didn't win the best-name prize, unfortunately.

But this choice of name also fits in with a theory on which these pages are based. We are not a semi-circle in search of another semi-circle, in search of completion.

Instead, we are Venn Diagrams: two circles meeting with an all-important, mysterious space in between, something that we each bring to the table, which nourishes the other person and – all going well – complements them.

The Venns are chefs who first encountered each other in the hot, steamy kitchens of Dublin's restaurants, so they know about getting the balance just right. Even more important because they are also lovers.

Too much pepper? It may make you sneeze.

Too much chili? You will burn your tongue.

Too much salt? It destroys the delicate interaction of the original ingredients.

Too much tarragon? Ditto.

Too much HP Brown Sauce? We may be too stuck in our comfort zone, unwilling to grow.

Too little of a vital ingredient? The relationship may crash and burn on the first date or – worse – over time become too bland and simply fade away.

Jennifer and Ciara have a lot to bring to a relationship. They're open and talkative. Opposites may, indeed, attract. In some cases, it's not always the easiest solution.

They live together with their cats. There's one thing their relationship doesn't need any more of: heat. They're together ten years and counting, chef together seven days a week in a restaurant they own and, this is the best part, they spar like crazy. They even went to the same school. (They were a year apart.) Neither of their yearbooks would have predicted this.

With good reason.

On the face of it, they couldn't be more different. The only thing they have in common – aside from their profession – is their sex. If it's true that we spend our lives looking for attributes we don't have, then this is it.

Jennifer is dark-haired and pretty – an old-fashioned, easygoing Irish lass, whose family originally hails from the west.

Ciara has a look of Jodie Foster about her: blonde hair, piercing eyes, a gravelly voice…and likes to give Jennifer plenty of lip. Ciara has a lot of fire in her belly. Jennifer smiles with resignation or rolls her eyes, when Ciara bubbles and comes close to overdoing it.

Ciara is Protestant, Jennifer is Catholic.

Ciara is upper-middle-class and holidayed in swish resorts in the 1980s when the rest of us were stuck in Torremolinos if we were lucky, while Jennifer was lower-middle-class and spent her childhood summers in Donegal.

Jennifer comes from a stable family background, which may account for her placid temperament. Her parents are still together and in love.

Her girlfriend's family is a different story. When Ciara was eleven her mother moved out and her father moved in with another woman who was nearly twenty years his junior. This moment, more than any, has shaped her attitude to relationships and may also explain her fiery temperament.

'I've no faith in long-term relationships,' Ciara says. 'Look at the stats: divorce, affairs, this, that and the other. I believe in the hippopotamus theory. Whoever the male and female hippo mate with becomes their lifelong partner. They hang around together, they're soulmates. The male takes care of his family but he does screw other hippos, in which case you can assume that she's getting screwed by another hippo. But there's no problem there because he comes home to her every night. I don't believe we could live like that in this day and age. But if we could wipe the slate clean as human beings, it'd be a better way to live because people change so much. I think open relationships are very healthy. They keep the family together, there's no bullshit. You've got to have respectful rules. But anyway, we don't have that and I'm quite happy not having that…Until I get bored!'

'She lets me know that regularly to keep me on my toes!' Jennifer adds. 'But, Ciara, I honestly believe that a lot of how you feel is because your parents are separated.'

'And all my parents' friends.'

Ciara's theory: 'You know why I think that is? Their tennis club. They go to play tennis and they shag each other after their G and Ts. A friend of my dad's said he didn't join the tennis club because he knew there was trouble to be had there. My dad used to have these huge parties. In one particular room, the lights would be down low and all the shenanigans?' Key parties? 'Just people flirting and a bit of a grope. And then they'd all end up splitting up.'

'It's not the tennis club,' Jennifer adds, 'it's the people!'

Ciara has a filthy sense of humour and a contagious laugh. Jennifer is an engaging presence but watches her Ps and Qs.

They both love the west. Jennifer summered as a child in Dunfanaghy, where she met Biddy and Barney.

They're both in their mid-thirties, wear nearly-matching but nearly-interchangeable woolly jumpers that look like they've been hand-woven in the Blasket Islands. That's one advantage of living with someone who is the same sex and – give or take a few curves – the same size.

Their restaurant is the type of 'in' place where gaggles of well-heeled, perma-tanned, blonde women in navy trousers and crisp white shirts go for brunch. With seascapes gracing the white-washed walls, the restaurant itself features from time to time in Sunday newspapers, as a place where the odd writer and TV personality hangs out.

They both like a few jars after work and on the afternoon we met they each had a pint of Guinness. Actually, they each had two pints of Guinness. They work long hours, fuelled with adrenaline as they manage demanding patrons and a large staff. Most relationships are pressure cookers without working in an actual pressure cooker. Were they polar opposites when they met? Was it firecrackers from the outset?

One thing they did have was chemistry. Lots of it. After a time, while they were still in their honeymoon period, the temperature hotted up outside the kitchen to such an extent that they decided to take a Thelma and Louise trip across Europe... in a 91D Toyota Corolla. They planned to begin their trip in France and finish up in Poland in a one- or two-year cross-continent trip.

'I had my period on the boat going over,' Ciara says, with characteristic frankness. 'I had my period on the boat coming back: that is, exactly twenty-eight days to the day in total.'

As Ciara explains, 'We were at each other's throats.'

'What pissed Jennifer off is that she'd see all these rich dudes on their golf buggies,' Ciara says. 'And that's right down my alley. It's posh and it's Quinta do Lago and it's nicely trimmed. It's not only a golf course, it's an actual area. It's very exclusive. And that's where I had my summer holidays. When I brought Jennifer, she was, like, "Oh, fuck this shit," and with the golf buggies flying around I was like, "Aw, so cute," and she was like, "Protestant bastards!" Which I am. Protestant, I mean.'

Ciara was a firecracker, a passionate, red hot fire cracker. Jennifer had her own quiet warmth, which was equally appealing.

Neither could be said to mirror the kind of relationships that they were brought up with. And although their upbringings were about as similar as Camembert and Gorgonzola, they didn't appear to be looking to repeat them.

When they came home and focused on their work again, something they did share, the holiday from hell faded into the background. They had survived it. They started a small catering service, which consisted of a computer, a car and, of course, some business cards. 'It gave us the Kindergarten, Fisher Price start-up pack for setting up our own business,' Jennifer says.

But being lovers *and* business partners changed things and the pots started flying.

'There were two leaders,' Ciara says. 'Then the killing started...'

WHAT'S LEFT UNSAID...
'My husband viewed gay sites and printed pictures.'

Dear Q

I am married two years. While using the computer months ago, I clicked on the address bar and up came several gay web sites. My husband has been logging on to them. I tried to put this out of my mind. Last week, he must have printed stuff off and he left a photo of a man from a particular site in his office beside the computer. I am gutted. I hate confrontation. Please help me. What will I do or say...

'Urgently Awaiting'

Dear Urgently

It's interesting that this didn't happen yesterday or even last week. It happened 'months ago' and yet you decided – understandably, I might add – to bury it, pretend it never happened, or tell yourself that there was some logical explanation. You said nothing. Perhaps your husband knew he left the URL unwiped, so when you'd type in a name with similar letters, these websites came up, perhaps he was being unconsciously careless or perhaps he was just plain sloppy.

But the fact is, when you didn't say anything the first time, he went ahead and printed out pornographic pictures and left them in his office beside the computer.

It's not like he pinned them on the refrigerator but he left them lying around all the same. He is either flirting with disaster and/or some part of him wants to get caught. Calmly, without judgement, present him with the information. You have hard copy. He, inadvertently or otherwise, provided it.

The issue of you finding it in his drawer or somehow crossing a privacy barrier is irrelevant. You could say, 'I found this.' And ask him what it means. If he refuses, you could say that you saw the websites before on the address bar but buried it. But the urgency of your email suggests that this information is dying to get out. Keeping these kinds of things bottled up can drive us to breaking point. You didn't ask me what I think they mean. I'll leave that for your husband to answer.

I will say this. Take heart in the knowledge that you have no choice but to tell him. As stressful as it may be, you have no choice. You say you hate confrontation. Well, this is a new beginning for you too. This is where you face those demons, you face up to problems and you stand up for yourself.

You've been married two years. You're young. Your whole life is still ahead of you, with or without this man as your life partner. It may not be easy, you may not like what you hear, but believe me when I tell you that when fear barriers are broken, we learn that we can withstand just about anything.

THE GAZELLE, THE WOLF AND THE EXOTIC BIRD #2

Six weeks after Michael and Robert's night out in the George, Michael is sitting in the Front Lounge, another regular spot, nursing a hangover, without Robert. He is single. Again. It's a while since he's been working out or practising his karate. Who took the currant out of your bun? I ask him.

'I'm getting a bit soft!' he says, repeatedly prodding himself in the tummy. He sighs. In the youth- and body-conscious world of Gayville, Michael, who is not yet thirty, feels that his body is beginning to let him down.

I never did hear how he met Robert. 'We met on the Net,' he says.

When Michael first knew Robert nearly three years earlier, Robert was too shy to meet him in the Front Lounge. He'd text him from outside and they'd go home together. It didn't take him long to overcome his shyness.

Now Robert has several gay friends his own age and ended up kicking his heels on the dance floor, while Michael stayed back minding the drinks, jackets and Robert's satchel from work.

Michael bought a house about a year ago, half-way through their relationship, close to his parents. Soon after, Robert moved in. 'We'd see each other first thing in the morning and at 10.30 in the evening. He'd go training after work. We'd see each other for about half-an-hour before we'd go to bed. On weekends, he was playing matches.'

'At twenty-seven years of age, I felt like an aul' fella! You need to be able to compromise to make a relationship work,' he says. 'But as much as you try, sometimes it isn't enough. Love isn't enough. And it's not a failing of anyone involved.'

Michael is run down. Daytime Michael isn't as perky as nighttime Michael, I offer. I wonder aloud if they'd get along.

'Get along?' Michael says, sitting forward with both hands on his knees. 'They haven't even met each other!'

We return to the aforementioned bun...and the missing currant. What happened to him?

A couple of weeks ago, he was beaten up badly in the laneway next to the Oak bar on Dame Street. 'I was taking a slash and the next thing I know I'm getting kicked to the ground.' He woke up in hospital. 'Everyone said, "Omigod, you've been gay-bashed!" Like it's this big thing. 'It wasn't because I was gay, it was because I was there.'

All this made him reflect on his relationships, his family and the recognition of his relationships by his family.

'All I ever ask is that they realise that my relationships are as emotionally important as anyone else's relationships,' he says. 'They can be as fruitful or dysfunctional as anyone else's. When I broke up with Robert, nobody said, "Oh, that's a shame." They said nothing. They still don't see it as a valid thing. It hurts. I'm going to write them a letter. I'm not going to bring it up with them face to face because I might get too angry. And in many other aspects of my life, they've been *very* supportive and defend me.'

We decamp to the Dragon. It's every man for himself.

Michael re-emerges a couple of hours later. He gives me a big grin as he tries to talk on his mobile. He mouths the words to me: It's Robert, his ex-boyfriend. 'Okay, pup,' Michael says quietly into his phone before hanging up. 'See you tomorrow.'

I didn't know they were still in touch. Like many gay men, they have managed to stay friends. Where heartbreak is concerned, Michael chooses not to remember – dwell – on yesterday.

'Where now?' he says.

Home? He's off to the Early House. He doesn't need a wing man. He thumps me one more time and gives me a hug. And with a fresh batch of friends to see the night out, Michael – the ever-hopeful gazelle, the romantic and the survivor – catches up with his friends. It will be a couple of hours yet before he sees home.

WHAT LIFE MAY COME
'I have dreams about being with men'

> Dear Q
> I have these dreams about me with other men, some famous ones, but I don't think I'm gay. Maybe I'm bisexual. How can I tell? Sometimes I get turned on by women and sometimes it's men but in a different way. Could it be that I'm unsatisfied sexually as I'm twenty-three and haven't had a proper girlfriend and don't get out much? Or could it be that at school I was teased and they assumed I

was gay because I was quiet and shy? Also, I seem to be attracted to the 'less manly' things – in life I mean. I'm a qualified florist and have no interest in soccer or other sports. I'm quiet, sensitive and shy. I never really was interested in girls but I put that down to being shy.

'Confused'

Dear Confused,

It's not up to me to stick a label on you and file you under 'g' for gay, 'b' for bisexual, 'h' for heterosexual or 't' for trisexual. Get yourself a tin of Campbell's Soup and see how easily the label peels off. Underneath, you'll find a silvery, shiny surface waiting without an identity. Tomato, minestrone or oxtail, anyone?

Many people experiment but that doesn't mean they will be forever branded with one label. There are lots of straight guys out there who like a calm, creative colourful life and many gay men who like a more active and sporty existence.

Your dreams mean what you choose them to mean. Perhaps your subconscious is experimenting with the vast possibilities that life has to offer but it wouldn't really be your conscious's cup of tea. Or perhaps your subconscious is trying to awaken all sorts of sexual desires to help you break free of your shyness. Once you gain confidence with time and life experience, or you meet someone who gets beyond your shyness, you will be in a better position to test-run your desires.

As long as being with or thinking about a guy/
girl feels right to you, go with it. And who says you
can't change your mind?

DREAMING OF HAPPY EVER AFTER #2

When mothers talk about their sons' rite-of-passage entry into gaydom, they invariably start with one subject: the coming out. When Aran, at sixteen, *tried* to tell his mother he was gay but couldn't blurt the words out, he made her guess. And guess she did. Martha feared the worst. She thought he'd been indoctrinated into a cult, or worse…

'I didn't know what to think,' she recalls.

When Aran arranged to meet his mam in the Bridge Bar on Westmoreland Street that night, he finally told her he was having 'relationship problems', and it took her another three hours, countless changes of subject and even more gin and tonics to guess.

As she left her house to meet her only son that night, Martha suspected that Aran had got a girl pregnant. He's a good-looking lad and wouldn't have any problem pulling. Plus, he's sensitive. Girls love sensitive. Martha asked her live-in partner, Simon, before she left, 'How are we gonna come up with the money for the abortion?'

Looking back, Martha shakes her head in exasperation. 'I thought he was shagging a couple of girls out of school *at least*,' she says. That night the guessing game began. Did he get a girl pregnant? Martha asked. No. Was it one of his teachers? No. Was he dating a famous person? (Nice try.) No. Did he join a cult? No. Long pause. There were probably only two options left. Was he abducted? (She appreciates that this was one last try before the inevitable.) No.

Did she say 'abducted'?

'I thought he'd been abducted by fucking aliens,' Martha recalls. 'At that point, I didn't know what to believe. And I didn't know what he believed. Anything was possible, including aliens.'

'There was one question left,' she says, locking eyes with Aran across the dinner table. 'I probably thought of it an hour before I asked him but I didn't want to ask him, partly because I thought if I was wrong he'd be upset with me. We'd been drinking for three hours. I eventually said the words.'

She asked him, 'Is it a fella?'

He nodded. A 'Yes' was his silent response.

They didn't talk about it for the rest of the night. Being in each other's company was enough. However, on the way home on the bus to Lucan, Martha got more upset, as the news finally took hold.

How could she protect him now? What about AIDS? The negative stereotypes? The prejudice? The hate crimes? How would he have children? Would he find love in the tumultuous, strobe-lit world of disco bars? Would life be more difficult for him now? Would other people make it more difficult?

When the bus arrived in Lucan, Martha was only beginning to realise just how momentous this evening was. How it would change her son's life for ever. By the time she arrived home, the initial shock had worn off and she could no longer hide her tears.

This evening, several years later, as we sit around her table with Simon and Aran, Martha's eyes glisten. Even now. She pours some wine. So she was surprised by her son's coming out?

'That's a fucking understatement!' Martha says. 'But I told him, stick with your pals, don't be on your own. I was worried that he'd have unsatisfying relationships. I was worried that he'd get his head kicked off him.'

Aran, after all, was still in school – a multidenominational school on Dublin's northside – but, unbeknown to his mother, he had already come out at school to his friends and, with the way rumours spread around the playground, the entire faculty.

'My advice,' Aran says, 'is to go on the gay scene when you want to go but don't let it take over your life.'

Martha says she does have reason to worry. If you're gay, she says, you *do* have fewer legal rights, you *do* have to put up with homophobic remarks, both in person and in the media. You *do* have more difficulty adopting children or even having them. You *do* get trivialised by a still staunchly patriarchal society that has an old boy's network ruling the roost.

What Martha, Simon and Aran have now is stability. They may not believe in happy-ever-after but they give it their best shot. No one joined a cult. No one was abducted by aliens.

And no one stayed in a bad relationship.

In the years since his coming out, Aran says he has 'loved'. He waxes on about relationships and how to make them work, a future with Mr Right, like any girl or boy his age. Unlike the gay generation that went before him, Aran has grander, more romantic thoughts to occupy his mind. He's had his dramas too...

One of Aran's previous boyfriends was controlling: 'It made me realise that you can really be in love with someone but it can turn into routine and, worse, dependency. It felt like I was married. I could have blinked and been forty.'

He's single again and has no problem with his status. 'If I was twenty-nine, I'd still be okay with it,' he says. 'I'd rather that than spend a lifetime with the wrong person.'

Simon couldn't give a flying fig-roll whether Aran is gay or not, as long as he is happy, and clashes with his stepson over other issues. 'The dishes,' Simon sighs. Some things never change.

'Martha hates ironing,' Simon says, lightening the mood. 'Yet she stretches and pulls and flattens the sheets, which takes almost as much time as ironing them.'

'I'll stretch, pull and flatten you if you don't shut the fuck up,' Martha replies, and goes back to meticulously cutting her cheese cake.

BETWIXT AND BETWEEN
'I love my girlfriend and my ex-boyfriend!'

Dear Q

I fell in love with the most beautiful girl you have ever seen and better still, she fell in love with me. Sounds perfect but nothing is ever simple and there are a number of problems. The first is that she is from a place far from Ireland and wants to move back there, and I'm not that sure. My business is growing.

We could delay it for a few years but I like Ireland and moving home and business half-way round the world scares the crap out of me. This problem, I'm starting to think, is the cloak for the other problem.

I've been out for over three years. I've always stated that I was bisexual but she was the first girl I was with in years. I miss men and don't know when it will pass. I was in a relationship, although a little unstable, for about one-and-a-half years with a nice young man, whom I truly love and – guess what? – the feelings were not returned.

We had broken up over six months before I met my diva. But after meeting him for coffee today, I realise I still love him. She has returned home so we can have a bit of space and time apart to decide what to do. She knows about my past and accepts it but I haven't said anything about my continuing male lust. I'm in so much pain that she is gone but I don't know if I could be true to her for ever.

Other than going to a monastery with eunuchs in Tibet, have you any pointers about how I proceed?

'Broken Man, Torn Heart'

Dear Broken

A couple of things are clear to me from reading your letter. You appear to be in love with two people at the same time – your ex-boyfriend more than your girlfriend? – which is made entirely possible because you are also a hopeless, dewy-eyed romantic.

You say your ex-boyfriend is not in love with you. Listen to him and stop chasing dragons. This also points a big arrow at how you feel about her. You love her but perhaps not enough, at least not now. You sign yourself as both a 'Broken Man' and 'Torn Heart'. I'd say it's the other way around.

You are a torn man nursing a broken heart. That being the case, I have a feeling that events will take care of themselves. Your ex-boyfriend will remain your friend, if only in your heart, and your girlfriend will move home if that is what she truly wants.

You may be in love with your ex and passionately love your girlfriend. What can *you* do? Tell her that she will always be special to you and, if you truly believe that you are still hooked on your ex-boyfriend, let her go. And if you don't follow her, you have your answer.

WHEN OPPOSITES ATTRACT #2

How Ciara and Jennifer communicated with the patrons in their restaurant helps explain how they communicate with each other and why they came home from their first holiday together twenty-eight days later. In the absence of meddling parents or pesky friends, Jennifer and Ciara had their grumpy customers to test the strength of their personal and professional relationship.

When customers complained, Jennifer, the happy home-maker, threw free food and a thousand apologies at the issue, and also held the belief that the customer is always right. 'It's a bit intimidating,' Jennifer says, 'how you dress, how you behave, it's a whole new ballgame really.'

Jennifer didn't have a talent for small-talk: 'If you listen to the waiters and the managers, they always say something very sharp, which causes a laugh and then they walk away,' she says. 'Whereas I get stuck at a table for twenty-five minutes and I don't know what I'm saying or how to stop it.'

'Simple!' Ciara interrupts. You say, "I have a pot on the stove and it's going to burn."'

When they bought the restaurant, they were given a gift by the previous owners: a voucher for Rathsallagh House in

Dunlavin, County Wicklow. It's owned by a friend of Ciara's mother. And, as Ciara says, 'It's very posh.' Mindful of their disastrous trip across Europe, which only got as far as Gibraltar, they decided that this was the perfect opportunity to chill before they got stuck into being full-time restaurateurs. When they'd taken previous weekend breaks, they'd usually book double beds at B and Bs but would always change their minds at the last minute.

They were a lesbian couple who wanted to share a room but – far worse for this self-conscious twosome – they were also voucher girls. Ciara says, 'When we arrived they were like, "*The Voucher Girls have arrived*!"'

They loved Rathsallagh House. 'You could have put a hockey team in the shower,' Ciara says. 'We were prancing around in our robes and...

'Let's just say,' Jennifer interrupts, 'it was very luxurious.'

For the first time, a landmark in their relationship, they stood their ground at reception, believing that to be voucher girls was far more shaming than something they had no reason to be ashamed of.

Ciara appreciates her partner, more than an outside observer will ever know. 'Jennifer has a degree, is an amazing chef, she plays the guitar, she plays the piano, she's an avid reader. Anything she does, she does it well. She's great at DIY. She's great at the English language.'

Jennifer suddenly gets serious too. 'I wouldn't have been able to be head chef if I didn't have Ciara working with me all the time,' she says. 'Like walking up behind me and saying, "Look what's going on in the corner," and walking off. It was like having a head-chef angel on my shoulder.'

They have many differences, stuff society obsesses about, such as class and religion. Even their similarities were not enough on their own to keep this particular Venn Diagram together. There were three ingredients that stood out: their sense of humour, shared sense of fuck-the-worldness and their individual strength. That is, they could laugh their way out of a disaster but they were not precious, damaged individuals who took anything the other said personally.

They fight, they argue, they laugh, they make up. They will do it all again because, ultimately, they are on the same team. And they know it.

Ciara wanted two more members of their family name-checked: 'And we've got two fabulous pussies! Write that: Barney and Gilmore. You can put their names in. We love to pet our pussies. People always say, "What are you doing tonight?" and I tell them, "We're staying home with our pussies."'

Which sets them off all over again.

FRIENDS LIKE THESE

They outlast most relationships and many marriages and frequently cause more trouble and strife. The friends you take with you on your journey play as big a part as family in your life. In fact, friendships can be almost as romantic as relationships.

Nowadays more people spend time playing house *sans* family, husband and three-piece suite. This generation gradually forged another kind of family, one the previous generation lost to nappies when they were in their twenties.

Today we have the non-nuclear family of friends.

Of course, like all families, they have their own peculiar dynamics, their power struggles, their tiny slights, their rejections and pain. They were supposed to be perfectly crafted, designed to replace the imperfect traditional family, weren't they? But we take our friends for granted too.

When Philip's wife died of cancer, he didn't want to see anybody. Then his two best friends from college arrived at his front door armed with wine and a week's worth of shopping.

He thought little of their gift until half-way through the week. 'I was in the midst of the funeral and the trauma when I realised how smart they were. I came home one night, completely exhausted. I opened up my fridge hoping for a crust of bread or the last mouthful of a carton of milk and there it was: filled with soups and ready meals and fresh fruit.'

Some have friends from kindergarten, who will see them through from their first kiss to their marriage thirty years later. At a recent barbecue I was introduced to a friend's niece. She was about ten years old. There was another little girl behind her, dressed almost identically but in different colours.

'This is my BFF,' the little girl said. She didn't need a name, just the acronym. Aside from her parents, this BFF – or Best Friend Forever – was arguably the most important person in her life. This is where she will learn about loyalty and camaraderie and they will have their first adventures together: going to their first disco, falling in love for the first time and, inevitably, having their hearts broken.

Sometimes, friendships turn into relationships. And vice-versa.

'Life may not be all watercolours on a Greek island with Labradors and grandchildren running around the place,' says Johnny, a forty-something writer. 'When relationships end, you have to make the decision whether to throw it all away or salvage what's left. Friendship is all there is. It's the gold that lies at the centre of all relationships, like scraping off the outer layer [the black enamel covering the jewels] of the Maltese falcon.'

Friends are there for births, birthdays, splits with boyfriends and girlfriends, the deaths of loved ones. You name it, they've seen it all. If your partner has run off with the au pair, your best friend will be standing in the wings with a bottle of wine and two glasses, or a Kimberley biscuit and a well-earned cup of tea.

TWO FAB LADIES #1
Maureen sits with her regular group of friends in the ballroom of the Seven Oaks Hotel in Carlow. She has light-brown hair,

an attractive, round face and a warm manner. She speaks in low, calm tones, carefully crafting her words. She also has a quiet mirth, falling shy of a nod and wink. Blink and you miss it.

There are only about 10 per cent men at the dancing. The women must be generous with their dance cards, dancing with women and men. The men, needless to say, do not dance with men.

Maureen and Angela come here to dance – they have won awards as a dancing team. But, for the most part, couples swap partners, married gentlemen giving time evenly to their wives and to widows, or to those, like Angela, whose dance-floor-shy husband has chosen to stay at home watching the telly.

Where are all the men? Maureen says, 'They're either dead or won't come.'

Angela, her tell-it-like-it-is best friend of nearly forty years, sits beside her. She has a frizz of brownish-grey curly hair, a narrow face and big rolling eyes that roam the room like a CCTV camera. She is the woman in the driver's seat who misses nothing. She could do a three-point turn without looking in the rear-view mirror.

Angela's husband didn't come; Maureen's died nearly twenty years ago. 'It's the worst thing that can happen, especially if you had a happy marriage like I did,' Maureen says. 'But I'm not interested in another relationship. I don't want to get bossed around!'

The first dance is up. 'The Yellow Rose of Texas' gets the punters out of their seats.

A tall dashing man glides by confidently with a woman in a polka-dot dress. They know what they're doing. A smiling Filipino gentleman whooshes with his partner, a grey-haired lady; they smile, speaking little, their feet doing all the talking.

She twirls her puffball skirt and it billows up in the air – an artful, dramatic piece of sartorial pre-planning. By day, this woman could be a librarian. By night, she comes out to play.

'We want something on the floor, Bernard!' Angela yells.

Bernard (no connection with Bernard Mustn't Grumble) sprinkles salt on the dance floor. Tonight, Bernard is single. (He doesn't yet know that he will soon meet a Russian lady who will make him the envy of the men at the ballroom dancing.)

'There goes Bernard, feeding the chickens,' Maureen says, as Bernard sprinkles the salt. 'You can slide on that much easier now.'

A woman twirls by with a man the size of Mickey Rooney on her arms. He appears unaware of the height difference. He is taking it very seriously. 'Look at *that* for a hip replacement,' Maureen says, proudly pointing at the lady.

Before I can get a closer look, she's gone around again. 'Men find it very difficult to come out to a place like this on their own. They can be so awkward to begin with but it's amazing how they build up confidence over time.'

This evening is proof that friendship abides, before, during and after your relationships.

'Life isn't over when you finish work, it's only beginning,' Maureen says. 'You need never be lonely. In our country, if you go for a job you're considered over the hill at thirty-five.'

The function room was the location for a small wedding reception earlier in the day. The reception is still going on, with an invisible wall between us. The bride, a robust woman with short brown hair, is wearing an off-white trouser suit paired with a pair of black ankle boots.

The lights dim. The atmosphere changes suddenly and dramatically. The ballroom dancing finishes up at midnight sharp so there is no time to lose. 'They turn down the lights to give the shy people a chance,' says Maureen.

The band starts up again with 'You Are My Sunshine'. 'They have to move very fast to get the partner they want,' Maureen says, as the men pick out their favourites. The dance floor, which was empty for a short break, is buzzing again.

Next up is the 'Paul Jones': women on one side of the floor, men on the other. Even the wallflowers get up for this one. It's more democratic, as everyone gets to dance a little and then switch partners. Maureen doesn't do the Paul Jones: 'There are already far too many women.'

Angela, however, is about to have a dance that will wipe the smile off her face. A mystery man is heading in her direction. Neither she nor Maureen have seen him here before and after tonight they never see him again. He has eaten something for dinner that has given him a potent, if temporary, bad breath. (Could it be chives or shallots? Bad for your breath, good for your prostate.)

The man heads in our direction. Angela hops up towards the bar. He makes his move and doubles back. Angela swerves around the table, to the left of the bride in the off-white trouser suit and black boots. But he is too quick for her. There's only seconds in it but he cuts her off. Angela is intercepted before she makes it to the bar.

'Look at Angela!' Maureen says. 'She does *not* look happy.'

Angela has a face like a wet weekend. She gazes over his shoulder with her head cocked conspicuously at a slightly awkward angle as if she had spotted a worrisome crack in the ceiling.

Her dancing partner does not seem to notice or mind. Here, diplomacy rules. While patrons have their regular dancing partners, few, if any, refuse to accept a dance. It's regarded as bad form. Still, I admire the man's chutzpah.

Angela flounces back to our table in a huff. Assuming we've seen her, she spits out, 'That...was...like...torture!'

Another gentleman asks Angela to dance. It's the 'Blue Danube' and, in order to feel the grand notes, Angela puts her chin in the air like a Russian Countess.

A man well into his eighties whooshes by. 'He'll give you Munchies,' Maureen says. What? 'You know? Munchies. Sweets!' she adds. 'Or a bar of chocolate. He's a Church of Ireland minister's son and he'll tell you about his record collection.'

A frisky man from the other side of the room follows the raffle tickets around, buying tickets intermittently, spreading his risk and increasing his likelihood of winning. (It works. He later wins several prizes.)

'We're best friends and haven't had a row in thirty-five years,' Maureen says of Angela. They must be very reasonable people. 'We are,' Maureen replies, adding in the same breath, 'and now we are going to dance!'

A man with a white beard jams on the synthesiser and sings into the microphone, his rich timbre lost on the room's harsh acoustics. Mickey Rooney flies by with his fifth partner, a tall, blonde woman. A charismatic couple – he in a suit, she in a black dress with a large flower print – swish by with their hands intertwined and raised high to the ceiling. They like to dance only with each other. Mr Shallots has another woman in his clasp, who appears to be in a state of suspended animation. Behind him, a woman in a grey pencil skirt and stripy grey tights and a man in a pink shirt clutch each other for dear life, spinning like a top. The smiling Filipino gentleman and his lady friend with the poofy skirt swan by with an elegant swoosh.

And, finally, best friends and award-winning dancers Maureen and Angela give it one more whirl in the crowd before the band plays out. They take off smoothly, the former leading, as they disappear, turning clockwise, into the kaleidoscopic blur.

MR MISUNDERSTOOD
'My friends won't admit not liking my boyfriend.'

Dear Q

I have been seeing my boyfriend for over a year. Although our relationship has had its ups and downs we have survived and are a very committed and loving couple. Neither of us has ever been unfaithful and we've always been honest with one another. My boyfriend has treated me with nothing but respect and love and he says he sees his future with me.

Unfortunately, my friends don't see this side of him. Even though they don't say it, they quite obviously dislike my boyfriend. This is partly to do with the fact that he is quite shy around them. He is also very insecure and has a bit of a wall up against people he doesn't really know.

It's got to me so badly that I have completely separated my friends from my boyfriend. I shouldn't have to separate the person I love from other people that I love. I've tried talking to my friends but they just deny that they don't like him. Can I look forward to a future with someone if there is such a big part of my life not involved?
'Unhappy Girlfriend'

Dear Unhappy

If you want your friends and your boyfriend to remain apart, you're going about it the right way. You're running scared and shielding your boyfriend from them.

This kind of protection won't help him to overcome his shyness in the long-run. At most, you could talk to him about why he thinks he's so shy and at the very least dignify the social skills he does have by allowing him to get to know your friends on a case-by-case basis.

This doesn't mean bringing him into a crowded bar and sitting him next to you in front of all your friends. That will only push him into his shell even more.

Try organising more intimate evenings with one or two friends at a time. Explain to your friends again, if necessary, or even casually mention your boyfriend's shyness in front of him, so you're all on the same page.

Your friends will hardly tell you they don't like him, even if they don't. They may mistake his shyness for sullenness or an unwillingness to get to know them. Separating him from them will only make matters worse. Start with your best friends and work your way out.

If your boyfriend has let you into his life, he's surely likely to lower the wall for your friends, given time. You're right. You cannot exist in splendid isolation. Your boyfriend may be drawn to the security of a relationship that is incubated from the rest of the world but it will do neither of you good in the longer term.

Explain to those involved not that you'd like them to get along better but that it's important to you that he gets to know your friends and they him.

READING BETWEEN THE LINES #1

It was the inaugural night of their book club and Celeste and Sorcha were having dinner in Gruel, chatting animatedly about their weekends. They were both distracted by a man but neither acknowledged it outright.

A tall, slim boyish-looking dude kept trying to earwig. He had brown hair, an innocent half-smile, a grown-up Jamie Bell look about him. Actually, he looks more like an older Jamie Bell than Jamie Bell.

They lowered their voices, finished their glasses of wine, packed up their bags and left. Who did he think he was? They were careful not to mention that they were in a book club. Marginally less taboo than MaybeFriends.com. They were not divorced, middle-aged women in their forties.

Not yet, anyway.

Celeste, a sunny blonde bombshell with an uproarious laugh, and Sorcha, a redhead with an even temperament, are both publicists. A book club on a Tuesday evening? They didn't want to publicise that. Their weekend had – in Celeste's words – been 'culturally virtuous'. Full of exhibitions and plays.

When they got to the Library Bar of the Central Hotel, they sat to wait for Kathy, Luca, a beefcake Italian charity worker, and Fred, an artist, schoolteacher and surfer. Celeste had chosen two women: Sorcha, her old friend from a well-known public relations firm, and Ruth-Ann, who also worked in the arts. Kathy, a writer, had chosen the men. It was an artsy-fartsy crew and a good start.

Celeste went to the bathroom and reapplied her red lipstick. When she came out she bumped into Fred, the late arrival. He was the eavesdropper from Gruel. 'I've been coveting your weekend,' he told her.

In his defence, Fred recalls of that night: 'We were all at the counter of Gruel, so I couldn't help but eavesdrop. It sounded like they both had the best weekend imaginable. It doesn't happen that often that you sit beside people in Dublin and say, "I want to be in their gang!"'

While other book clubs fade due to lack of commitment or dissolve because of an opinionated member who makes everyone else's life a misery, this was a success. It is now in its third year. They had lively and heated discussions and, very occasionally, sparks would fly. Each week, they met in different venues around Dublin, the Westbury Hotel one week or Romano's Italian restaurant on Capel Street the next.

'We were scared of one another at first,' Sorcha says. But they persevered.

They discussed Brian Merriman's *The Midnight Court* and Iris Murdoch's philosophical manifesto *The Sovereignty of Good*. Some fared better than others. One month Sorcha chose *The Reluctant Fundamentalist* by Moshin Hamid about a Pakistani man in a post-9/11 world and it did not go down so well.

They spoke about passion, love, betrayal, metaphors, ethics. They also brought a lot of their own lives to their work: their own disappointments or dealing with the death of a loved-one. The themes of the books leaked into the lives of those in the book club.

After a year, their little group expanded to include a gay television producer, who had a love affair with books and briefly had a fling with Celeste's best friend, and the wife of a prominent politician, who would make the gang laugh with funny stories about Bob Geldof and the Queen of England. Luca, the Italian, met a woman and went off to raise his children but Sorcha and Celeste stayed regulars.

They had a real barney-brack over Michelle Faber's *Under the Skin*, a book about a cannibalistic female hitchhiker with a penchant for muscular men.

Sorcha said, 'Why are you being so reverential about the book?' She felt there was a double standard afoot. Sorcha is a vegetarian. The others are not. She felt personally about the carnivorous/cannibalistic theme and believed strongly that there was a connection between the two. That night, unfortunately, they happened to be having chile con carne. All except Sorcha.

Fred, perhaps because he's a teacher, was able to navigate the club back to harmonious common ground. Celeste saw this. And more. She. Was. Impressed.

'We were discussing *Wuthering Heights* one month,' Celeste recalls, 'and I said, "Who'd marry boring old Edgar Linton when you could marry Heathcliff?" Fred put up a good defence for poor old Edgar. 'He defended the good guy. And he's not a Heathcliff. He's not a bad guy.'

Fred remembers, 'I didn't quite get the attraction of Heathcliff. He was a tosser. I couldn't understand why literary types like Celeste would go for him. I'm not as big a lover of literature as she is. Edgar seemed to be the all-round good guy. Heathcliff was just mean.' He also confesses, 'I started reading it the day before and ran out of time so decided to get the DVD, the Lawrence Olivier version.'

Judith Earle's *Dusty Answer* provided another challenge. This time it was Kathy's choice. Kathy, a lively brunette in her forties, is a writer and producer, and from another era. She is untouched by the grimness and plastic conveniences of modern life.

'When you call Kathy up, she is usually marinating some chicken or putting some fresh fish in the oven,' Celeste says. 'You'd never find her eating a McCain's Oven Pizza.'

Something else started to happen. Talking about epic themes of love, loss, innocence and sexual awakening started to change the way Celeste saw things. She began to see things she'd never seen before. She found herself looking at Fred...in an entirely different way. 'It made me more romantic,' she says. Strange for a book club that had one unwritten rule: 'No Chick-Lit'.

Back at the book club, everything appeared normal. Fred was still willing to shake it up and experiment with plays and poetry. 'He'd have us all reading Archie Comics if we let him,' Celeste says. Each month, Fred was the first to go. One week, he had to see a man about a canoe. Another week, it was something equally random like a surfboard.

It slowly became apparent that the only remaining single straight man in the group was not like other men. And he was quite the catch, surfing in Lahinch on long weekends, teaching the nation's children, creating art that was deeply personal, rather than epic statements on war and peace.

One night, after Fred had gone, Sorcha suggested setting him up with one of her single friends. They would make a good match. Celeste was not happy. 'Why would you do that?'

For the first time in a year-and-a-half silence fell in the book club. Not because they were shocked; they had been waiting for this to happen.

KISS BEFORE LYING
'Should I pretend to be my gay friend's girlfriend?'

Hi Q

I'm about to start my first year at University College Cork. One of my good friends from school is doing the same course as me. Over the summer, he told me that he was gay but he hasn't had any experiences with another guy. I actually quite fancied him but I have tried to be supportive. Now that I know he's gay, he's more like a brother. His parents always thought we were an item, even though we were just friends. They'd always ask me to family events. And if they went out for special occasions they'd ask me along. We placidly went along with the boyfriend-girlfriend notion. We are in a platonic sense, anyway.

But here's the problem: he has tried telling his parents that he was gay. He even hinted once that he was bisexual. But they went ballistic. His mother cried. And his father said, 'Don't come back into this house if you really believe that.' So he played it down since them. Out of sight/sound, out of mind...that kind of thing. Now, he wants me to go along with the charade. He says it's just continuing the way we were. He also wants me to kiss him on the cheek the next time we see his folks. I think, considering his recent attempts to come clean, it's rerunning a fictional story that has no happy ending. His parents don't live near Cork, so it's easier this time.

I don't want to be dishonest or hurt anyone. What should I decide? Help!

'Childhood Sweetheart'

Dear Sweetheart

I'm with you on this. I don't believe kissing him in front of his parents to allow them to believe a fiction is the way forward for any of you. They know deep down but they're obviously willing to pick up and run with any signal that he is a red-blooded Irish male heterosexual. The fact is, he's a red-blooded Irish male homosexual and is doing himself no favours by burying his head in the sand along with his parents.

He does want to buy himself more time, however. And, as he does live with his parents, that's perfectly understandable. Make it clear to him that this is a temporary arrangement. Let him drop your name into his telephone calls home, if he wants. But I wouldn't further the charade. It will only make it worse when the truth comes out. And, considering his previously brave but foiled attempt…out the truth will come. Eventually.

THE NOT-SO ODD COUPLE #1

Danny and Alex are an imperfect couple. They met in the small ads of the *Village Voice* and shared a tiny apartment, a third-storey walk-up in New York's Lower West Side, for five years. Danny is a multi-tasker from Setauket in Long Island with a string of get-rich-quick schemes; Alex, originally from Galway, is a writer, more serious than Danny.

Alex left Ireland shortly after graduating from Trinity in 2000. He decided he would live a little, maybe write a novel – or two. He is six feet four inches tall, with jet-black hair and dark, soulful eyes. Danny is half-Italian, short, stocky and soft around the edges, like a rugby player crossed with a teddy bear.

While Alex crafts sentences and sweats over his art, Danny goes for robust good cheer: 'If you laugh the world laughs with you,' he says, 'if you cry, you cry alone. Am I right? Am I right?'

Alex doesn't answer. He takes a deep breath, one beat short of a sigh, as Danny falls around laughing like one of those mechanical clowns you might find in a fairground in Coney Island.

An elderly gay couple lived on the ground floor of their brownstone in New York. If they met in the hallway, one or other of the couple would usually holler, 'Hiya kids!' even though they were both well into their twenties.

Danny thought nothing of it. It made sense to him. He was a big kid, after all. Alex felt a sense of foreboding at the remark. He knew that one of these days the 'Hiya kids!' might stop. And then where would they be? Two men sharing an apartment with not so much as a career between them.

They did bug each other from time to time. Danny would read ten pages of a book while he was in the bath and leave the book in the bathroom. Alex would pick it up, dry it off and say nothing. Danny cooked a great spaghetti Bolognese, which he learnt from his Sicilian mother. Alex did a mean washing-up, which he learnt from his.

Like Ciara and Jennifer, they are opposites. But Alex and Danny are not a couple. They are just friends. The small ad they read was of the 'Single Male Looking for Roommate' kind. Their life together was better than any pre-marriage course. They each learnt to tolerate the other's domestic shortcomings and to pull their weight.

Their apartment originally had one bedroom, divided by a piece of plywood disguised as a wall. They shared a windowsill. They could wave at each other before they went to sleep. It was not soundproof so they kept a jar of earplugs handy.

'My friendship with Alex is a safe haven,' says Danny. 'That's a key thing with all my really close male friends. Even if you screw something up, even if you're wrong, they don't judge you. When stupid shit happens, you know what the other person is living so you can forgive it. In fact, forgiveness isn't even necessary. It's more like, "Oh, that sucks!" There's no score sheet or tally.'

'The cliché that guys don't talk about feelings gets over-played,' Alex says. 'There is a way of resolving things by bolstering each other without actually talking about the issue at hand. It lets the person know they will always have that basic connection. The repressed Irish male gets a lot of bad press. As does the shallow American.'

Alex listens to the Smiths. Danny still overplays Blink 182. The name of the first girl they fought over? 'Brooklyn Diane,' Alex says, 'and she wasn't interested in either of us.' Their favourite holiday destination? 'Honolulu,' Danny says; 'Laos,' says Alex.

It's a Mr and Mr with a twist. They may not be married or romantically involved but for those five years they were a couple.

'I do think an awful lot of male behaviour has to do with expectations of what the male role is,' Alex says. 'Things that are written into the role from a very young age, such as not revealing vulnerability and being resolute about decision-making. That unyielding behaviour isn't the best kind to have. The language of that world, of fighting your corner, tends to be quite male, framed by dominance rather than cooperation.'

Over time, they broke this mould: Danny with humour; Alex with quiet patience. Danny has another take on it: 'Alex arrived in New York in 2000. That experience of emigration was probably hard for him. He moved to New York at a young age, perhaps before he had fully defined himself. He was uprooted. We did the last part of our growing up together, establishing a career, navigating our way.'

Danny doesn't think his prankish ways are unacceptable to Alex. 'There is a certain one-upmanship in male friendship. There's a kind of measure of character in how people can handle being flagged…' Slagged, actually. 'Slagged! Or ball-busted, as we say in America. In female friendship, there is more acceptance and spirituality. You want a male friend who minds your back. If I was an astronaut I'd be looking for someone who could get me back to the station.'

Danny and Alex didn't go to space together. As if almost sharing a bedroom for five years wasn't enough, they decided to sublet their apartment and go on a round-the-world trip together, a trip that might make or break their friendship. This trip ended in Dublin and changed both their lives.

MY FRIEND, THE SCROOGE
'She arrived for dinner with a six-pack of Twix!'

> Dear Q
> There's no easy way to say this. My best friend
> from school is a Scrooge. She arrived for dinner
> at a mutual friend's house recently carrying a six-
> pack of Twix. But that's just the tip of the iceberg.
> She prides herself on not drinking or smoking,

which is admirable, I agree. But I know part of this is to save valuable moolah. She's becoming an embarrassment and, quite frankly, I'm finding her difficult to handle. Should I accept her as she is?

'At Wits End'

Dear Wits

Stinginess is one of the worst qualities to put up with in a friend, family member – or anyone for that matter. Not least because it's usually the tip of the iceberg – selfishness, meanness of spirit…The upside is that the Twix incident provides a funny story that will keep you going for weeks.

But this is only fun in the short-term. It hurts to see a friend betraying her true qualities and tarnishing her good name all over town. Who knows the reason for these quirks. Perhaps she grew up in a house where saving pennies was deemed the key to success. Perhaps she's already saved enough to set up her own graphic design company and will surprise you all. Or, perhaps, as you say, it's just plain rudeness.

Either way, if you are friends and you wish to stay that way you have two choices: tackle the issue the next time it arises (micro-approach) or tackle the 'Scrooge issue' in its entirety (macro-approach). Try the first. If it doesn't work and you think the stinginess warrants it, try the latter.

But remember this, if the macro-approach provokes a backlash, which can happen when any of us are faced with the Awful Truth about ourselves, both of you may realise that your once-valuable friendship is worth no more than thruppence. But, addressing the issue with humour head-on is the only way to find out.

TWO FAB LADIES #2

In the half-light on this smoggy evening, Phibsboro could be a suburb of Tallin or Moscow. It seems like an unfamiliar land: the foreign accents and austere concrete shopping centre. There's something else odd. It is like that scene in *Chitty Chitty Bang Bang*, the city without the children, only this time it's the other way around. There are no elderly people.

At Doyle's Corner, opposite Kelly Carpets, is Phibsboro Library and behind that is the St Peter's Scout Hall, which hosts bingo on Monday nights. Once I get close to the muddy laneway, the scene changes. I spot a trickle of little old ladies – and they are little – in overcoats and sensible shoes, shuffling like penguins in the one direction through the smoggy, cold night air.

The scout hall is dark and empty at 7.30 on a Monday evening. Betty flicks the light switches on in the kitchen, which she has pretty much done for this not-for-profit bingo night for the last forty-five years. She has short fair hair, a beige sweater and a white blouse with a stencilled flower in the middle.

Although Betty turns up week after week during school term – the scouts use the hall during the summer holidays – she insists that she doesn't much like bingo.

'I have to be honest,' she says. 'Bingo is not my cup of tea, not in a million years.'

Her friend Peig is quieter but has been on the bingo circuit for twenty-five years, most of that time as Betty's right-hand woman. She defers to Betty and kick-starts stories for Betty to run with.

They were neighbours: Betty on Emmet Street and Peig close by on the North Circular Road. There used to be seven of them, a group of friends who got together and kept the bingo up and running. Now, there are two if they're lucky, sometimes three.

The original seven were Betty, Peig, Kathleen, Betty D., Kathleen S., Eileen and Nellie. Some have died, others drifted away because of circumstances or ill-health.

Kathleen was found dead at her home by her relatives who were concerned that they couldn't get through to her. 'She was sitting at home with her knitting. If you had a cold, she'd be in with an aspirin and a bottle of Lucozade.'

'In our time, growing up around Emmet Street was lovely,' says Betty.

Betty, a widow, and Peig, who is married, talk of jewellery shops and antique stores behind Moore Street, the old Ambassador Cinema around the corner and Nelson's Pillar.

There was a turning point. 'It all went downhill when Nelson went,' Peig says, lamenting the day they ever put up that spire. 'They should have put St Bridget up there or something.'

Peig's shocking white hair is in a pony-tail and scraped back off her face, on which a warm smile appears to be permanently etched. She wears a pale-blue fleece, a sensible choice since it's raining outside.

These days, there are not so many places for them to go. Hence, the bingo. It started as a fundraising enterprise for local causes nearly fifty years ago but now they're used to having it around.

A gaggle of golden girls gather outside the door of the scout hall having a smoke. In school, these elderly friends would have been behind the bike sheds. They are well into their sixties and seventies, some wearing girlish pink tracksuits, influenced by TV and their daughters' wardrobes. They take deep drags on their cigarettes, cackle, murmur, wheeze and burst into regular roars of laughter. A woman with thinning grey tufts of hair talks about her daughter, who she suspects won €10,000 in a larger bingo hall after she arrived on her doorstep with a load of cleaning products, but has kept it a secret.

One lady takes out three packets of Tayto crisps and places them neatly around her table. These are set places. Their ticked boxes wait for no man. A large woman, one of the last, rushes through the door. 'I wasn't born in a hurry,' she says, snapping up her Bingo Book for €3.50, 'I'm Irish not Rushin'.'

There's no big money here. It's €3.50 to play. For the ordinary cards, you get €5.00 for a line and €10 for a house.

'It's a lot more in Cabra,' a tobacco-soaked voice in the darkness outside the hall says, 'that's why I gave up going.' There's a round of tuts to follow that one, as if a flock of noisy pigeons just passed overhead.

Betty has had to fight to reduce the fee from the council to use the old scout hall on a nearby site and then to have the new hall built in its current location: 'They said we weren't industrial, we were domestic.'

Peig, sitting opposite, nods supportively: 'I remember that!'

'We'd have a sale of work to make money to pay for the bingo in the hall,' Betty adds.

Peig flies the flag for her friend. 'She got this one built!'

Betty pauses but takes the compliment. 'That's quite true,' she says evenly. 'Somebody called me up, looking to buy the old hall. I said, half-joking, 'How much would you be able to give us for it?' And he told me and I said, 'You'd want to put a few noughts on the end of that!' You know who it was?' I shake my head. 'It was Mountjoy Prison. We did a deal but they had to build us this hall when we sold the old one.'

I take a seat, which is padded. A woman with jet-black hair approaches: 'Sorry, love, I'll have to take that chair, if you don't mind. I've got piles up the you-know-whats.'

I hand it over.

The bingo begins. 'The Luas line…number nine,' the lady on the stage says. 'Half way there…45,' she adds. And on she goes, faster and faster. 'Leaving school at…14.' All heads are down. 'Almost there…89,' she says. 'Who says so?' a rebellious voice cries out from the back.

Bingo keeps you in a heightened state of anxiety, as you're always on the precipice of winning. The ladies at the next table have a packet of Oldfields and Werther's Originals, which they spread across their table in their wine and gold wrappers, rustling and sucking as they spike each number with their biros.

As more women get closer to winning, there are gasps and sighs getting more frequent and audible, as two lovely ladies 88, or legs 11 (there'll be a reliable whistle from the back for that one, every time it's called out), or two little ducks 22 (there'll be a 'quack, quack!' from someone else for this to help ease the stress of being just one number away from a full line). Then, there's a self-satisfied 'Check!' and the room erupts into more sighs, more tutting and gabbing in a mass decompress.

The first 'check' means somebody has a line of numbers across. The second 'check' means a full house.

As we start to cross off the numbers on our last bingo card, the table of six women to our right put on their coats without standing up. It's a deft manoeuvre. They start to pack away their sweets. It reminds me of school, when the final bell was nearing.

When the first 'Check!' is shouted into the cavernous, concrete hall, they zip up their coats and put on their scarves. One more full house (and 'Check!') and they're out that door.

Betty, Peig, the woman with the piles up the you-know-whats, the lady whose daughter may have won the bingo and the rest have structure, routine, companionship, entertainment, gossip and the odd fag. And they have friendship. When there's no one left at home, they have everything they need right here, in the scout hall at the bottom of this laneway in North Dublin.

FABULOUS FORTIES
'My married friends only ever try to set me up.'

Hi Q

I turned forty last month. I had a fabulous birthday party with friends from school and all parts of my life – some single, some dating, some married and one widowed. It was a wonderful night and I thought, 'I've done okay. Life is pretty good.' But once the candles were blown out and the guests went back to their respective homes, everything went quiet again. I've had two long, wonderful relationships. One bad one. I'm happy to take a break for now but the invitations have dried up. And less than half the people who attended my party even called to say, 'Thank you.' Why don't people ask single women to dinner parties (unless they're arranging a blind date with some overdone turkey). I always make the effort with my married friends. Why don't they with me?

'Cheesed Off!'

Dear Cheesed

Gee whizz, I would be too if I were you. It sounds like you need to put the word out that you're more than an even-numbered stand-in for your friend's single friends. If they're good enough friends, they can take some straight talk: gentle but firm. It'll be a good test to sort out the wheat from the chaff. It doesn't mean they cease to be your friends. It means you must look elsewhere for your social whirl, because as much as your closer-than-close friends might love you, people lead busy lives. They just need to know that when they have the time, arranging a dinner party with Mr X is not the way to go. But you should take the initiative and invite/drag your favourite girl/boyfriends into your world, too, whether it's going to the opera or checking out your favourite late-night watering hole. Remember, it works both ways.

READING BETWEEN THE LINES #2

Celeste turned a new page: she invited Fred to an exhibition at the Dorothy Cross Gallery, then they went for kebabs afterwards in Zaytoon. Like you do.

They were finally socialising outside the book club. They got along great. But they were still friends. Friends with a twist. They flirted with each other and went on friendship dates. They were stuck in no-man's land. They were having a friendationship.

'I was also seeing somebody,' Fred says, 'but the relationship was at an end. It became like a date. I hadn't consciously decided anything at that time. I had such high esteem for Celeste. She wasn't the sort of girl you could get involved with casually. It had to be a respectful serious relationship or nothing. As I got to know her I really liked her.'

Celeste invited Fred to be her plus-one at a wedding. Originally from Limerick, he is a gentleman at heart. 'I realised that I couldn't be going to weddings with one girl and still be going out with someone else.' He split up with his girlfriend. He was now single. Bingo! (Sorry, wrong story.)

They went to a Franz Ferdinand concert with Fred's Italian flatmate, Massimo, who asked them separately, 'Why don't you marry each other?' Massimo didn't even suggest a date. When he saw them together, he aimed straight for the altar.

'I remember deciding then that I was prepared for this to be a serious relationship,' Fred says. 'I told myself, "I am prepared for this to work out or not work out."'

Still nothing happened. How would she tell him? After all this time, over a year in the book club, Celeste had suddenly realised she'd fallen into the pages of one of the chick-lit books that were banned from her book club. Fred, of all people. The cute surfer, schoolteacher, artist and Jamie Bell lookalike. Like, what the hell would she do, like?

For all her talk of Irish Murdoch and Ernest Hemingway, all her pontificating about Judith Earle and Moshin Hamid, Michelle Faber and Emily Brontë, she had become a character in cheesy romantic fiction…and Barbara Cartland was her fairy godmother. Worse. She had not fallen for the rogue Heathcliff, but for Edgar Linton, the nice guy. Maybe it was about time.

It was nearly Christmas, and Celeste had set up her own business and moved into new offices on George's Street. Fred called around with coffee, pastries from La Maison des Gourmets and incense. This was the moment. It was speak now or never be at peace.

They chit-chatted. Her blonde curls bobbed with anticipation. But for all the conversations about love and death during their book club, she couldn't free herself from the small talk. Other friends arrived to help her celebrate. They saw Fred. They were excited to see him as they knew this was the night Celeste would make her intentions known.

They looked at him. Fred looked back. He looked at Celeste. Celeste looked at her friends. Without over-dramatising, it's fair to say that they were pretty much all looking at each other.

One of her friends said, 'Did you tell him?'

'Tell me what?' Fred said.

Celeste changed the subject.

Fred had plans. And he left.

'I'm coming with you,' Celeste said.

It was down two very steep flights of stairs.

'Coming where?'

'I've got to talk to you.'

'About what?' Fred really wasn't getting it.

It was snowing on George's Street. They stood on the steps of the building.

'I really, really fancy you,' Celeste said.

He did something very subtle but it made everything seem right. He placed his hand lightly on the small of her back and said 'I feel exactly the same way.'

One-and-a-half years, eighteen-odd book-club sessions and several friendationship dates later, they were finally dating.

They walked to Café Bar Deli. Fred had to meet a man about a kayak. Celeste was going to the opera. Just your average Tuesday night.

'What do we do now?' she asked.

'We go on a date,' Fred said.

They met outside the Gaiety at 11 pm.

Fred had ordered a private room in George's Bistro on Baggot Street. They had visited Hemingway in Paris and walked with the Brontë sisters on the Yorkshire moors. The way they read books and shared stories and the way they saw each other had irrevocably changed.

He proposed in London. In a diner. A greasy diner. In the East End. And it was perfect.

'I whipped out a box hat I'd spent hours making,' Fred says. He placed it on the table, waiting for her to notice. But the waitress came with Celeste's coffee and it was terrible.

'Celeste hated it! She told the girl to bring it back, the waitress was quite rude and they started having a fight over the coffee and I sat there with my box and eventually I had to cough and bring her attention to the home-made box on the table and eventually she realises I'm about to propose.'

And she said, 'Yes.'

'We didn't hang around the crummy little diner too long,' Fred recalls.

Celeste preferred it to a mountain. 'The greasy spoon. The sausages and eggs. Perfect.'

'We weren't the sort of people who were going to lose themselves in a wedding,' Fred says. 'For us, weddings were like Christmas and the real meaning of Christmas was obliterated by nonsense. We wanted the commitment and the essence of it. Neither of us wanted to get married in a church but we found this great priest and a great church, just off Grafton Street, which was strategic for Celeste.

They had a wedding lunch in L'Gueuleton on Fade Street. There was more drama to come. 'My four-year-old nephew split his head open in the middle of that,' Fred says. 'He fell over his sister's buggy. He was rushed to the hospital. There was a lot of blood.'

That evening they had a reception in a house on North Great George's Street. The bride wore raw silk, fire-engine red, like her lipstick. Barbara Cartland would probably not have approved.

HARD NECK, SOFT HANDS
'I went to my friend's for dinner. She insisted I wash up!'

Hi Q

I have a friend whom I've known since we were about twenty-two. We're thirty-two now. We've been through college, our first jobs and countless relationships, supporting each other all the way. My friend, let's call her Mary, has always had an edge or funny temperament. But it has been getting worse. She's always pushing me into corners and I don't know how I got there.

A while ago, she invited me around for dinner as I was stressed out over work. I went around, she cooked a beautiful meal. I was very touched. But then she said, 'I cooked. You can wash up.' There was a mound of dishes. It's as easy in some ways to cook for one person as it is to cook for two. I felt she invited me around to do the washing up. I did it but I resented being tricked into it. She's always doing stuff like that.

Nothing is just for the gesture. It's always tit-for-tat and it makes me so mad I could strangle her.

'Marigold'

Dear Marigold

I'm glad to see you haven't lost your sense of humour. No doubt you need it, especially after an evening of enforced washing up. Your friend may be as great as you think/hope her to be but she's certainly acting dishonestly. Friendship is based on love, affection, compatibility and other qualities that are wholly unconditional. From what you say, your friend demands compensation for every little thing she does for you.

She is passive-aggressive and controlling and shows more than a little meanness of spirit. I'm not surprised you have a hard time getting a handle on this dirty pot.

Mary pulled a fast one the other night. There's no goodwill in a gesture that requires payback. Worse than that, to offer it and then take it away so brutally is both cruel and hurtful. Sounds to me like she's on quite the power trip.

However, I think you should wait for the next opportunity. It's never wise to store up past experiences to unleash all at once. You're not trying to win an argument, remember. You're trying to save a friendship. Plus, Mary could say, 'I was kidding.' Or, 'You're very sensitive.' Or, 'I can't believe you felt this way all this time.' Or, 'Hands that do dishes can feel soft as your face.'

This meanness is premeditated. You have to make a stand. You have to tell her that she's got to change her ways. Sometimes, you have to risk losing something in order to keep it. The confrontation probably won't be pretty. Remember this: You're thirty-two, not twelve. You don't need this kind of relationship in your life, so don't let her soft-soap you.

Strangling her won't solve anything, even if you wear rubber gloves. You'd do a lot more washing up on the inside.

THE NOT-SO ODD COUPLE #2

Alex the writer and Danny the joker lived together for five years in a cramped New York apartment. They couldn't get enough of each other, clearly. So they decided to up sticks and travel the world together.

On the first leg of their trip, they landed in Hawaii amid the honeymooners, then on to Tokyo, Australia, Vietnam, Thailand and Laos. There was a short stopover in London to see friends and finally Dublin. So did it make or break them?

'Danny is a close friend, but it's a completely different thing spending time with each other day-in, day-out,' Alex says.

That doesn't sound good. But there's more…

'I found that Danny was a person I could spend the rest of my life with. There was no tension whatsoever. There were lots of frightening situations where we didn't know where we were going, where we were lost in the dark in the back of a tuk-tuk [rickshaw] travelling into nowhere, but we didn't once blame each other. I can't think of anyone else, close friends or family or wife, about whom I could say that there would never be any tension. I have friends of thirty years and I would be climbing the walls with them after three hours.'

And Danny Boy? How was it for him? 'The trip was the best thing we could have done together.' In fact, the closest they came to disagreeing was on the final leg of their journey, when they were navigating the London Underground. But they survived.

When they moved to Dublin everything changed. Alex met a girl and got married last year. Danny also decided to stay in Ireland permanently and settle down – with Alex's sister.

'Living here has given me a taste of what it was like for Alex those years in New York,' Danny says. 'We arrived back in Dublin three years ago. I now know first-hand that the experience of being an emigrant makes you ask, "Who the hell am I? What the hell am I?" Am I right? Without the support of a good buddy, people could go zoom, just veer off the rails.'

'Male friendships get slightly dogged with beer-swilling and back-slapping,' Alex says. 'But the core of any relationship is a shared regard for the other. This is not gender-specific. The killer in divorce cases, where counsellors throw up their hands, is where one person has contempt for the other. It doesn't take much contempt to destroy a relationship.'

'I now live in a small house with lots of noise and a high level of stress,' Alex continues. 'Going out for two hours and sitting in the company of a friend, not even talking very much, is very restorative. This space is very important to men. Without this outlet there is major scope for boredom and frustration to build up, which turns into depression.'

Having been in Ireland for nearly three years, Danny sees differences between Irish and American women. 'Most Irish women work, have careers, yet they spend three hours preparing a roast-chicken dinner on a Sunday, just for me, all for me,' he says, licking his lips. 'Certainly in America you find women who love to cook, but the evolution that brought them to have a career would have weaned them from the traditional part of keeping a home. Irish women have kept a huge amount of what their mothers taught them and it's no big deal. It seems like they've managed to keep both sides.'

'In Ireland there seems to be a stronger tie in marriage,' Danny adds. 'In America things are more fickle. I know people who have been married four times. That would be unheard-of here. Here, the idea of having your man is important. Everything has to be equal, housework and raising kids, but it doesn't have to be the same because men and women are different and do different things. What's nice about Ireland is that I can talk about that difference without being considered a male chauvinist or anti-feminist.'

They don't always see each other as much as they would like but when Danny marries Alex's sister, they will officially be family. Danny says, 'I might call Alex up and say, "Are you sure it was in Big Nick's that we met Brooklyn Diane?" We have the ability to lighten up each other's day with about five words. Alex has been a lifeline for me. He was this island where I could stand for a minute and say, "I'm not a fish. I'm a human being." Then I regain perspective and know that everything is cool.'

'When we meet, the conversation just resumes,' Alex adds. 'There's little in the way of small talk. You pick up exactly where you were. Being polite would undermine that. For us, the conversation never really ends.'

6

Why We Choose Those We Do

Some women like strong, rude, gruff men who will thump an annoying bloke who hassles them in a bar. Men might like an equal-opportunity sparring partner, a lamb to protect or someone who makes them laugh.

Who has the power? Who is in control? Most are better off when it's 50/50, a healthy, constantly revolving tension of wants, needs…and compromises.

Some people like blondes, others chestnut-browns, some tall and leggy or short and stocky, hairy or smooth, fair-skinned cailíns or dark-skinned Lotharios. Often we surprise ourselves when we choose against type. All the time.

Most of us are looking for love but don't always know how to recognise it.

'I got married twice,' says Bernie, a fifty-something secretary. 'I wanted to be with someone who was the polar opposite of my parents.' And? 'The first time I married my father. The second time I married my mother.' Come again? 'My father was cold and distant. My mother was neurotic and insecure. Despite all my best efforts, they were the two personality types I was drawn to.'

Like Bernie, we sometimes search for love in all the wrong places, date one emotionally distant partner, learn our lessons, find somebody else, then wake up one day to find that partner number two is so far away emotionally that he/she might as well be living in Alabama or Timbuktu. We don't want to repeat past mistakes but nobody is baggage-free.

A popular theory about choosing partners is that we repeat relationships we had in our formative years. If we are used to being treated with a certain disdain, chasing after affection that remains tantalisingly out of reach, we will continue to do so.

Crazy love with conflict and strife and drama and tears can be entertaining and make us feel like we are living but pain can also be addictive. This could be why some people continue to make bad choices, seeking out good-for-nothings who will give them their next hit.

In relationships, we are the stockbroker, the stock and the investor rolled into one. We put a value on our own stock. We are who we want to be. When we become that person, the idea is that we will attract people who find independence and self-worth attractive qualities in another human being.

The qualities we seek in others we should also exhibit ourselves. So the next time, ask yourself, 'How was I so lucky to meet this thoughtful, sensitive woman?' Or, 'Why are all the men I date creeps?' Be warned: if we seek an impossible perfection in others, we should be equally demanding of ourselves.

HE WHO LOVED YOUNGER WOMEN #1

Richard, fifty-seven years old, looks down at his cappuccino with interest. The cream and chocolate froth swirls around the cup until it forms a love heart in the centre.

'If you tried to do that you wouldn't be able to do it!' he says. We're sitting in a noisy coffee shop in Dublin's Epicurean Food Hall under a skylight that allows the sun to beam through. He wears his years remarkably cheerfully. He's divorced. 'I see myself as just single.'

He's about 5'7', slim rather than athletic – the way he describes himself when he looks for love in the personals – and is wearing a black leather waistcoat over a grey shirt. He has thinning grey hair parted at the side and geeky oversized glasses.

He's also remarkably confident.

He does not want to meet a woman his own age. He's not deluded, exactly. He doesn't look in the mirror and see Colin Farrell or Cillian Murphy staring back. He sees Richard. And that's good enough for him.

He's not shy and he knows what he likes: Women under forty-two, slim women, photography, poetry (he has won a Dublin poetry competition), hiking, adventure, Latin America and his two daughters.

He knows what he doesn't like: smokers, women who are not slim, women who are over forty-five, women who have let themselves go, matronly women, women with children, meaningless sex, status symbols (that includes women in SUVs), women who go on and on about their ex-husbands or ex-boyfriends, his job in an electronics laboratory, people who take him out of context (though he admits he can be blunt), his ex-wife and – there's one more – the wife of the man his ex-wife had an affair with. He is harder on her than the man who had sex with his wife.

Other than that, he's all ears.

Richard married in 1975.

'People were more innocent then,' he says, gazing into the middle distance. 'I had the attitude, you get married and everything works out fine.'

That didn't last long. His wife had an affair with a local man.

What's worse, he was the headmaster of the local school. Worse than that, it was the local primary school.

'I discovered the affair,' he adds. 'I woke up one night and I had a flash of insight. Have you ever had a flash of insight? I get them occasionally.'

He'd remembered the night his wife came home and told him that she'd joined the school board. 'There was something embarrassed or scared about her. Then I watched them together. I knew they'd been having an affair. Then I discovered a letter he wrote her, which she kept in a drawer.' He adds, 'She was a very calculating woman.'

But judging by where she hid the letter, not a very smart one. He didn't care much for the headmaster or the headmaster's wife. 'The headmaster's wife was mortified when she found out,' Richard says, now giddy. 'She was a real bitch, she only cared what other people thought.'

He didn't feel the need to move: 'I still live in the same house. I was the aggrieved party. I could stay whereas she couldn't. They can think what they want, I don't mix much in the community.'

He separated from his wife in 1987 and they subsequently got a Catholic annulment. 'We had to fill out all these psychological reports for the annulment. One covered immaturity at the time of getting married,' Richard says, stirring his cappuccino and messing up the frothy heart. At the time they met, he was twenty-eight. She was twenty-two.

He last met his ex-wife at the christening of his first grandchild. She had a man on her arm (it was not the headmaster): 'We're civil. I wouldn't say we're friendly.'

His last relationship, several years ago, was a 'healing experience'. He was forty-six, she was twenty-three. 'It happened accidentally. We were in a walking club. She's a lovely girl.'

Richard, a sprightly go-getter, if that last relationship is anything to go by, doesn't like women his own age. He believes he's more active than most women of his age and doesn't feel his fifty-seven years. Hence, the leather waistcoat.

He is, by his own admission, a particularly chauvinistic specimen of the Irish male. But he is not alone.

Men can date a woman for five years in their thirties without any pressure to pop the question and, then, without warning break it off and go on to have another five-year relationship. Their relationships never grow older. Like Richard, they feel as young and carefree as during their first one.

Richard wants to clear something up. He values his independence. He needs no one. 'I am not your typically conservative Irish male. I value family and friends and appreciate the needs of others and am not a mammy's boy. I can use a washing machine and cook a meal. I am very a good listener and a faithful friend. I have two wonderful daughters, both living abroad, and we get on really well. I recently completed a degree in humanities and now I am learning Spanish.'

He does want to meet a woman but, after you hear what he has to say about Irish women of a certain age, he'll be lucky if there's one single woman of any age left in this country who will want to meet him. Still, he's willing to take that chance.

YOUNG MAID
'Where's the knight in shining armour?'

> Dear Q
> I have been single for practically two years after breaking up with someone I was going out with for six years. I moved to a small town in the west of

Ireland to start again. It might sound very dramatic but I knew that I'd never get over my ex if I stayed where I was and I was offered a good job.

Initially, it was great crack being single and I'd be the first to admit I loved the thrill of sleeping around but this thrill didn't last much longer than six months. I started to feel cheap and like a sexual object so I decided to hold off on the passion until I met my husband.

I used to joke that I'd never meet anyone but that joke is not funny any more. Any men that I do meet are married or in relationships or five years younger than me and not in the market for anything serious. I am starting to get a very bleak impression of men. My parents are happily married and my ex was a great guy so I'm starting to think that I just got very lucky with the men I've been close to. Some friends' boyfriends have suggested that I am too picky for my own good but honestly I feel I broke up with a great guy so why should I settle for someone less than him?

I'm not looking for George Clooney but I do need to be attracted to someone and I am picky when it comes to personality. I am shy but am told I scrub up pretty well. I have lots of great friends and I think I have a lot to offer.

I'm generally quite happy with my life, and would love to find someone to share it with. I just seem to be attracting the wrong kind of guy and can't find the right one. People always say I'll meet someone when I least expect it but I have been waiting around for this knight in shining armour for too long now and he has not arrived on my doorstep.

Am I setting my sights too high?

'Currently Celibate'

Dear Currently

Underneath the shining armour, when the knight has stripped off and left his helmet and sword on the bedside locker, you will find a man of flesh and blood who is real and will have needs and faults and desires. This knight will probably have an overdraft, gambling debts, issues with his parents, be tired of travelling horseback all day long and his legs are killing him and why does he always have to be the one doing the jousting and why didn't that comely maiden return his advances and he probably smokes too…in bed.

That's the thing about knights. They're great when they're in uniform but just wait until they get you up on that horse and bring you home. And I haven't even got to the paunch yet, and the receding hairline and alimony payments to that princess who said she had a dowry but it turned out her father's castle was mortgaged to the hilt and she hadn't a bean, not even a magic one.

Just meet the blokes, talk to them, enjoy the gifts that they have to give you, take the good, weigh it up with the bad. And don't wait for the knight in shining armour because you may find yourself spending a lifetime trying to polish it.

PUTTING HIS EXES BACK TOGETHER AGAIN #1

In light of all the above, it is no surprise that some women are willing to make compromises. Enter Matthew. He is tall, friendly, still has his own hair, is nudging thirty-five and, for a man who has only recently started playing the field, has been landing himself a hangar full of attractive, smart, intelligent, women. He works in science. He earns a good living and has a permanent job, even though he won't be president of the company any time soon. Or at all.

He has an innocence about him that both women and men find appealing. He is at home with his sexuality. He was shy in his twenties and is like a teenager in his thirties. He's just as happy if a guy fancies him as if a girl does. But he will only kiss the girl. He once kissed a handsome guy and, while he appreciated his beauty, he didn't like it.

Matthew is not what you would call classically handsome. How does one put this delicately? Matthew puts it best. 'I have been told that I have a head like a boiled egg.'

But don't hold the egghead against him. Nobody else did. 'I grew up in Waterford and had a relatively strict Protestant upbringing,' he says, 'My mother taught me to respect women and I respected them so much that I could never take it any further than friends.'

Then he kissed one of his female friends, a girl he worked with in his first job. They went out, then broke up, not because they didn't get along any more but because he discovered something about himself that he hadn't realised before: except for the odd fumble in the jungle, he'd spent his twenties as a virgin. And now he was as horny as hell. 'In my thirties, I wanted a second chance to live my twenties. I wanted to see what I missed out on. I was too young to settle down.' So…he didn't.

That's when the *Gospel According to Matthew* took a turn for the better. He has managed to date far out of his league.

Matthew had what we might loosely call charm, which got him through the bedroom door. It came to him easy.

Matthew was filling the void for sexy, vibrant women who wondered why they weren't appreciated by Irishmen. When men did woo them, they turned into stay-at-home-slobs or on-down-the-pub-likely-lads.

The difference between Matthew and other Irishmen is that he loved women, openly and boldly. He was like a child in a candy shop. If a beautiful woman walked passed him, he would smile at her like an adoring little boy, turn his head, feel his heart race, even that familiar stirring in his groin. He was finally embracing his sexuality and felt pure joy at seeing an attractive member of the opposite sex. Before he could help himself he would simply say, 'Hello.'

It wasn't a strategy exactly. It was just something he did. The women he wooed were tired of drunken slobs stumbling up to them in bars with the first cheesy chat-up line that came into their heads: 'Would you like a drink?' Or something to that effect.

In the far corner, we have women who are more educated, better-dressed, more moneyed and confident than any previous generation of Irish woman. They are getting married later in life, in their thirties rather than in their early twenties like their mothers. By the time they've established themselves in their chosen profession by the age of thirty-five they have maybe five good years to meet a man who would make not only a good husband but a good father, date for a respectable amount of time in order to get to know him, move in together, get married and/ or have X number of children. That's a very tall order in five short years. 'Time is against you,' says Emily, the girl who left her farmer's heifers in the dust. 'Men smell our desire and our fear like a cheap perfume.'

In the near corner, we have men who are also educated, moisturised, brush their teeth, get them fixed, veneered and/or whitened if need be, shave, dress smartly, act polite and chat up girls like Emily with questions rather than talking constantly about themselves. These men know what women want: it's a metrosexual-heterosexual hybrid. Why settle down at thirty-five when you've got time, money, sexual freedom on your side? Who wants to give up the twice-yearly skiing trips with the lads? Why not wait until your late thirties or early forties and marry a woman who's ten years younger?

At the edge of the ring, running around like a puppy dog in heat, is Matthew. What his future girlfriends didn't realise, however, was that there would be a downside to Matthew's puppy-dog eagerness. At first, he seemed like that rare male: unconventional, open with his emotions, always laughing, never boorish and always adoring. But for every positive aspect of being emotionally immature, footloose and fancy-free, there was another one that would soon come back to bite them. He was a snapper. This is something his ex-girlfriends, who have queued up to tell their tales, would discover only later on.

A FEW GOOD MEN
'Do Irishmen disguise bad behaviour with charm?'

> Dear Q
> Having lived in a number of different countries, I
> have an observation to make about Irishmen. They
> are among the most charming and attractive males

I've come across but are utterly untrustworthy. It doesn't seem to matter whether they are in long-term relationships or not, they still chase women. They don't admit this, of course – you just sort of find it out. Or, even better, you just presume that every male you come across is in a relationship, until proven otherwise. Any comments? Do you agree/disagree with this?

'Hung Out to Dry'

Dear Hung Out
Best consult a few female friends on the subject. This is straight from the horse's mouth:

Lady Luck No. 1 (38), happily married to an Irishman: 'In my experience American men are more untrustworthy. Have faith and stop being charmed by the players. Hang back a little bit and look out for a quiet, shy type of guy. Be honest and true to yourself and hopefully you will meet someone who will treat you with the same respect.'

Lady Luck No. 2 (36), happily living with an Englishman: 'I dislike these sweeping general-isations about Irishmen. I find them hackneyed. The problem isn't nationality, it's simply gender. All men are untrustworthy, except mine.'

Lady Luck No. 3 (29), happily single, with a child: 'Perhaps their mammy's-boy mentalities make them better at being convincingly honest than their brash European counterparts because they are aware that they'd be hung out to dry if discovered playing the field by their women.'

So there you are. The views from three different women show one thing: generalisations are influenced by your own experience. We all find different qualities attractive, whether it's wide-boy antics or the soft sell.

It all depends on the individual and the choices we make as individuals. Yes, there are too many wild boys on the loose but there are still a few good men.

THE GIRL WHO DATED FOREIGN MEN #1

Helen was used to helping friends who had the weight of the world on their shoulders. She had recommended hairdressers and dentists, tailors and electrical repair shops. She has advised her friends about their wooden teeth that needed a little whitening but only when they complained about them.

Helen was nothing if not polite. She only ever wanted to help other people, not insult them. Even in her work, her focus in entirely on other people. A former model turned stylist, it was her job to make men look effortlessly handsome and women look pretty.

Helen has naturally blonde hair, long eyelashes and sallow skin. As a girl was thin, even though she ate three balanced meals a day. She went to a private non-denominational girl's school.

She spent her teenage years and early twenties in west Cork. Her late father was an English Protestant engineer, her mother an Irish Catholic interior designer. They lived in seven different countries before she was fourteen. When they returned to Ireland, she was sent to boarding school.

'I was the typical outsider, one degree removed from every pop-culture reference.'

With glittery eyeshadow, her love of gold sparkles and green eyes as big as saucers, she looks otherworldly.

Her unusually thin physique and model looks didn't always go down well in school. 'They used to call me the Alien Autopsy Experiment,' she says.

Maybe that's why she always dates legal aliens.

Now in her thirties, she is the type of woman who turns men's heads in the street. She is quiet in large gatherings. She is usually a listener, not a talker. She is an anomaly in modern society in that she appears more interested in other people than herself.

José Carlos, the Brazilian artist, was full of plans. He was a swarthy young man of exotic beauty, another alien orphan in this land. She met him in a gay bar. Naturally, she thought he was gay.

He squeezed her behind and said, 'Nice...'

She laughed. Gay boys are so fresh. She squeezed him back. He was there with his gay friend, he told her, but he was straight. 'Can I squeeze it again?' he asked.

'No,' she replied. Still, the ice was broken.

'He had the cocky air of someone who had achieved all his plans,' Helen says. 'I think he told so many stories about what he was going to do with his life that it didn't matter any more to him whether he did it or not. He was living off the fruit of his dreams rather than the fruit of his labours. Fact and fantasy got all mixed up together and that's where he decided to live, in a world of unrealised dreams.'

Helen did fall hard for him. But he wasn't ready to settle down. José Carlos moved to New York and gave her two weeks' notice.

Andy, the self-styled London aristocrat from a housing estate in Wandsworth, lasted two months. He needed to find himself.

'I was really fucked up,' he says of their relationship. 'My parents put me in boarding school at the age of twelve. I never recovered from that. I felt like a dog they didn't want any more. They didn't have the heart to put it down, so they sent it off to the country.' He doesn't have enough money for lunch. 'Can I borrow a tenner?'

Helen says later, 'He asked you too?'

He still owes her €300.

Stefano, the Milanese banker had a heart of gold but spent all his time preening himself in reflective surfaces and didn't have room in his life for another relationship. There were three people in his life already: Stefano, his reflection in his bedroom mirror, where he checked out his skinny jeans and winkle-pickers and leather jacket, and his reflection in the hall mirror, where Helen says he pouted and practically blew himself kisses before he left the house. One man, two reflections.

She should have known. When she brought him to a family wedding, he jumped around the dance floor, slapping the rear end of his jeans: 'You like my ass? You like my ass?' Thwack! Thwack! She did. As did her Aunt May and cousin Hilda. And about a dozen other women on the dance floor at the time.

One day, he told her he was being conscripted into the Italian army. The letter had come. He had to do his time. There was nothing he could do to prevent that. There would be no tears at the airport. One morning, he got up from her bed, kissed her goodbye in his skinny jeans and left.

Three weeks later, she bumped into him in Whelan's. 'How did he think he would get away with it?' she says. Did he ignore her? 'No.' Did he make up a story? 'He did not even do me the honour of that.' Did he blush to the roots of his hair? 'He didn't even flinch. He appeared happy to see me.' Was it awkward? 'It was too surreal. It was like seeing a ghost. Part of me was glad to see him. The other part was confused.'

Did he try and get away as fast as his skinny jeans could carry him? 'Worse.'

Worse?

'He wanted to come home with me.'

Next up was Ben from Paris, an IT consultant in his early thirties who dreamt of becoming a film director. 'He did a lot of night courses,' Helen says. He was a real piece of work himself: sombre, quiet, sexy and very, very boring. 'It's difficult to express just how boring he was,' Helen says. 'I don't remember any of his stories. Nothing. Hardly a thing. Either he didn't have any or I have blanked them out as a form of self-protection.'

Ben jacked in his job and went back to Paris. 'My theory,' Helen says, 'is that there he could imagine himself as a character in a real-life movie that he would never make.'

She never broke up with any of them. Even when she felt like it was the best course of action. They always beat her to it. She was hopeful. It was not a bad thing. She wanted to see the good in other people even when it was hard to find.

'That's what I told myself. The truth was I never spoke up, I never lost my temper, I never put myself first,' Helen says. 'I spent time listening to them go on and on and on about their lives, like that was what women were put on this earth for, to listen to them dream. But I never listened to myself.'

She had finally had enough. One morning, she awoke and could barely get out of bed.

And that's how Helen sleepwalked her way to her therapist's office in Ranelagh on a rainy Wednesday afternoon in November, sat alone in the living room of a period house, listening to the whispers in the next room, doors opening and closing, until finally her name was called. She dated all these gorgeous foreign men who didn't treat her right. The question now was: why?

THE NEXT BIG THING
'I'm sick of self-obsessed guys in their twenties.'

Dear Q

I've been playing the field and meeting guys for what seems like a lifetime. Actually, come to think of it, it *has* been a lifetime. I'm in my mid-twenties. Most of the guys I've dated have been around the same age as me. But they all seemed so self-obsessed, so wrapped up in their looks, sex appeal, car, career and, most of all, their future. It's always been about them, them, them and I'm sick to my teeth of it. I'm tired of boys who don't know their own mind.

Do you think I should aim a little higher age-wise? Men do mature later than women and I think if I went for someone in their thirties or even forties, I'd have more luck. Wouldn't they be more settled, have more formed characters, be less concerned about what people think of them? Wouldn't that be the best chance I have for a mature, lasting, adult-to-adult relationship?

'Sick of Babysitting'

Dear Babysitter

You're right about one thing. When you date someone who is on-the-up, full of a sense of their own potential, you take on the role of casting agent on whom the sexy, wannabe stars-of-tomorrow test their best and worst lines. If you're both on the same trip, it can be worth every moment, even if you have a return ticket. But when you're looking for more stability, sensitivity, empathy, you're right again: it's time to say, 'Thanks for the enthusiastic pitch. Now leave your CV at reception.'

Age has everything and nothing to do with it. While we spend our twenties trying on different personae like shoes, we'll find the same qualities with men and women in their thirties and forties: they may have picked up a smidgen of arrogance on the way, if they're overly happy with their lot; or a dollop of bitterness, if they're not.

Age and/or experience can teach us but, alas, how emotionally well-adjusted a person is does not depend on a number.

HE WHO LOVED YOUNGER WOMEN #2

'Women over forty are like my aunt,' Richard says. Loudly. 'I don't visualise them trekking in Peru. I'm not prejudiced against fat people but Irish women are letting themselves go to hell. They're rapidly becoming gross. I wouldn't say that to a woman, I'd get a slap. It's probably partly genetic. They have a longer lifespan. I know a woman who died at ninety but didn't do anything except shop from when she was forty-five to the day she died.'

We are still in the café in Dublin. A guy in his twenties, eating a club sandwich at the next table, twitches but looks straight ahead. Richard is on a roll. 'One of my problems is I'm blunt and

I say what I think. I get misunderstood. I'm much more tolerant than I appear. I've no hang-ups. I have no problems with gays. I only have a problem if people think me and my gay friend are a couple. Gay people have great walking groups. They're very organised.'

He met a woman online who drove a Lexus jeep. 'I'm not into prestige.' But is it because she has a nicer car than him? She may just like the jeep. 'I can't change who I am. I have to have some sort of criteria.' These criteria also rule out women who have children. 'I've raised my own kids, I don't want a woman with children trailing after her.' What if they were grown? 'Then she'd be older. She'd have to be at least fifty.'

His love of younger women raises eyebrows. 'People think men like me who look at younger women are perverts. I said to a female co-worker, who's thirty-two, "That woman has a lovely figure." She said, "You have a daughter!" And if I had displayed interest in her sister she wouldn't have that either.'

Richard recently returned from hiking in Peru with a male friend, who is gay, and three women, who joined them after they advertised in a local newspaper for travelling companions to split the cost. 'One of the women was very disagreeable: she didn't want to do anything we did and bullied the other women.'

They didn't stay in touch when they got back home.

Perhaps his award-winning poem showcases his more sensitive side. Please note: he said if I use it, I must use *all* of it. He is not one to be edited. It needs to be read in its entirety, so make yourself comfortable. He would like it to be credited with his Internet *nom-de plume*, Steppenwolf.

IMAGINE

In another life,
another place,
in a dusky room
peopled with grey
   shadows,
I play jazz trumpet.

Laying the notes down
smooth and crisp
brassy and arrogant,
gifted with brilliance,
to emerge triumphant
in a mellow breeze of
   praise,
like a mountain stream
crashing earthward
in a giddy vortex
of unrepeatable
ecstasy.

Or like a perfect evening
melting with honey
on a tranquil lake;
where notes
like silver fishes
dart and dance
to a score unaltered
for a million years.

Or warm and gentle,
like making love
on rainy afternoons,
scented and sweet
as rose petals
scattered on a dewy
   lawn.

And sometimes
with an aftertaste
that lingers on the soul
rather than the lips –
whose kiss on brass
   reshapes
my world of dreams.

Oh, my. For all his brash exterior and potentially offensive opinions, the man has hidden reservoirs of sensitivity – deep, deep, *deep* down. To his credit, he's not interested in one-night stands, which makes him a rarity among men. 'I've too much in my life without wasting time trying to get laid. I'm choosy. I've turned down many one-night stands. I've felt there are too many strings attached. You'd have to phone the next day and blah, blah, blah.'

'Don't get me wrong,' he adds, 'I had a fantastic sex life with my last girlfriend but it's not the be-all and end-all for me. If Britney Spears was here and I didn't like her, I wouldn't care.' He thinks about this a moment. 'But I might make an exception for Kylie Minogue.'

Has he ever thought his criteria were too rigid, that women under forty might mostly prefer men under forty, that despite his own active lifestyle he's unlikely to be asked to grace the front of a chocolate box anytime soon? Has he wondered that women may find him a little – to say the least – chauvinistic? A friend of mine says older men like younger women because younger women are less likely to know whether a man is good in bed or not.

Richard isn't insulted. On the contrary, he's amused. 'I haven't had many women fighting over me so I haven't had the opportunity to play them off one another. I'm not bitter. I'm just cautious.'

There is something vulnerable and honest about him, despite his views. Off he goes, back to work his last days in his laboratory before his retirement, with his goggles and white coat. He is all bravado and bluster, yet few people know about the poetic beast of a man who lurks within.

GIRLS WHO LOVE BOYS...WITH GIRLFRIENDS
'How can I stop falling for men who are taken?'

Dear Q

I don't know if I go for boys who have girlfriends
subconsciously or whether I seem to attract boys
who are already taken and just want a bit of fun on
the side. Either way, lately these are the only guys
that I seem to date. There have been three in the
last six months. The trouble is I've kind of fallen
for one and as much as I like to think he'll leave
his girlfriend for me I know he won't. I don't know
what to do. What advice can you give me? How
can I avoid boys with girlfriends altogether?
       'Living Dangerously'

Dear Danger

You can avoid them by asking yourself why you
choose them to begin with. Because whether or
not you are gaining a reputation as a girl who loves
other girls' boyfriends, you are choosing them.
Because you can always say no, you can always put
yourself in the girl's shoes and think, 'If I were her,
what would I think of me?'

What do you think of you? Do you think
you are not worth a fully-fledged monogamous
relationship? Are you afraid to try for one in case
you experience personal rejection? Are you angry
with the world for some other reason?

Or do you want the most valuable commodity
on the market? And what could be more valuable

than a man who already has his qualities trumpeted by a current girlfriend?

Do you not trust your own judgement? Are you the type of girl who wants that beautiful dress in the window if: (a) it's priced out of your range; (b) has a designer label; and (c) comes highly recommended to you?

It's time to put some faith in your own judgement. Sure, a dress with a celebrity endorsement might be just as appealing as a boy with a girl on his arm endorsing him. But, as you've found to your cost, just because they're spoken for doesn't make them worth having. Not if they're so ready to cheat.

PUTTING HIS EXES BACK TOGETHER AGAIN #2

If Matthew walks down a street anywhere in the world, women don't do a double-take. 'I never got that kind of attention,' he says. 'I gave them all the attention.' They needed to get to know him to appreciate his gifts. If any of his ex-girlfriends were to walk down a street in Rome, Paris, New York, they'd get wolf-whistled or a second-take from male admirers. Men give them the lights. Not so Irishmen.

Emily says, 'Who do they think they are with their pot bellies? The ugly bastards! They expect to go out with Eastern European supermodels who are stick-thin! Look at all these beautiful women in Dublin who are single and all these ugly bastards turning them down.'

Everyone except Matthew, that is. Matthew dated girl after girl after girl. Not just any girl. Sexy girls. Intelligent girls. Successful girls. Glamorous girls. Women. After a drought that lasted most of his life, he is now in the right place (Ireland) at the right time (2008). So he slept with lots and lots of women.

He loved them all. Other studlier men would now look at him from afar and want to hang with him. They could never come close to landing the kind of girls he landed. They were square-jawed, probably more interesting conversationalists, had bigger egos, were more overtly confident, yet they were his wing men? How did he do that? Why did this small army of women fall for him? If you ask them why, their answers are revealing.

'He was persistent,' Emily says. 'He'd leave in a taxi and, when everyone else was gone, he'd come back again. The doorbell would ring and he'd be standing there with a big, stupid grin on his face. He pursued me, like no Irishman I'd ever met before… or since. It's difficult to describe just how he wouldn't give up. He was your friend but just when you least expected it, he'd be all Hands Christian Anderson! But with him, it was the clumsy advances of a poor boy who should know better. And it was a compliment. He did what other men could never master. He made you feel sexy and special.'

'Matthew was fun to be around,' according to another girlfriend, at least at first. 'He had a wide-eyed quality about him. Like this little boy in a sweetshop. He was very sociable but there was a childlike warmth about his manner. He didn't grow old and boorish, he stayed young and impressionable. He'd make you feel like you were in some kind of screwball comedy. He could get away with it because he seemed so harmless. He was always laughing. That's how I remember him, laughing his big head off, all the time.' He did something else that struck her as unusual. 'He always listened to what I had to say.'

But when he tried to settle down, Matthew wasn't the catch he appeared to be. He successfully compensated for his lack of sexual experience with sexual adventure for a time but he was only papering over the cracks. He never dealt with his own deep-rooted insecurities because of spending his teenage years and twenties without a proper girlfriend.

'It was a nightmare,' Emily recalls. 'I think a lot of Irishmen don't try very hard. I wasn't even that crazy about Matthew. He just wore me down until he succeeded. There's something about a goofy guy who hangs around to prove himself.'

Matthew moved into her house. He became jealous, constantly clicking on her latest Facebook Friends, calling into her voicemail, accusing her of carrying on with other men.

'That's when he changed. He became controlling and pushy. I think he has a dark side; he's a real Jekyll and Hyde. I think something must have affected him as a child for him to be like that. He was searching for acceptance through his relationships with women. At heart, he was distrusting of the world. He kept moving on. How could he really love you if he didn't love himself?'

But another ex-girlfriend, Paisley, the optimist who was unfailingly polite, went easier on him and thinks of their time fondly. 'He wasn't a player, a mover or a shaker. He was not a calculating man. He didn't see any boundaries. There was a lovely innocence, an exuberance about that.'

DREAM LOVER, WHERE ART THOU?
'Something's up with the man of my dreams.'

> Dear Q
> I'm going out with the man of my dreams but although I thought I'd be ecstatic about this relationship, I'm not. We were going out previously for about two-and-a-half years. Then we broke

up but because we had the same group of close friends we always ended up together at some stage or another. We had a baby together about sixteen months ago. And, after it being off for nearly three years, we got back together. I was delighted, of course, because he is my best friend too and also a great father.

But there seems to be something missing. I'm an affectionate person and liked to be touched. I send nice messages and that sort of thing but I always seem to be making more of an effort than he does. He was totally different when we were going out last time and I know people change. But I'm unsure if he does really love me or not. I know he does still find it hard to show his feelings after we broke up the first time. But I don't know whether that's an excuse or whether he can't treat me like his girlfriend. I'd appreciate some advice.

'Unsure About Our Love'

Dear Unsure

I recommend that you not put your partner on a pedestal by looking at him as the man of your dreams. (And, in this case, wondering why he won't stay up on that damn pedestal.) You could tie him to that pedestal and swing him till he's too dizzy to undo himself but he'll fall sooner or later.

As he is your best friend and a great father, he's certainly going to be a fixture in your life one way or another. It seems you're both finding your feet after an on-again, off-again affair. The biggest clue to what's going on at the moment probably lies in the reason you broke up with each other in the first place. He may be with you for a myriad reasons. The fact that you share a child could be one of them. But whether this is love, I can't tell you.

A lifetime ago a friend gave me the most bizarre piece of advice ever. She asked, 'Does X love you?' I shrugged and said, 'I dunno!' It wasn't something I'd thought about. What love is to one person could mean something totally different to another. But my friend wasn't happy. She looked me in the eye and said sternly, 'I think you should find out.'

Find out? Find out what, exactly? Had I embarked on this quest, I would have felt like Indiana Jones searching for the Lost Ark. After a period of time, a relationship either satisfies your needs…or it doesn't. If it's the latter but you think you're both on a learning curve, give it time. You're jointly raising a child and that has got to be tough. If your boyfriend has told you that he's finding his feet, again, I'd give him the space to do just that.

THE GIRL WHO DATED FOREIGN MEN #2

'I longed for puppy fat and spots like the other girls in school,' says Helen. 'My misfortune was that I didn't have them. That set me apart from the rest.

When I started modelling part-time the girls in school called me Skeletor. It was preferable to being Alien Autopsy Experiment.'

Why not Irishmen? 'About half the Irishmen I've slept with

– and there haven't been that many – couldn't get it up. Actually, more than half.'

And foreign men?

'Never had that problem.'

Ever?

'Never.'

'They are so sure of themselves. They know they're exotic creatures in a strange land.'

A bit like Helen. An Anglo-Irish Princess who felt imprisoned by her beauty. A modern-day Helen of Tory.

Helen wanted to know why she chose these foreign men. Why they always had to be other-worldly. After her last break-up, Helen wanted answers. This is why she found herself at the therapist's rooms in Ranelagh.

Her therapist said her name softly as he popped his head around the door. Marcus, she would decide over the coming months, was a lovely man: understanding, warm, sexy.

'You should always fall a bit in love with your therapist,' she says.

'Helen…' Marcus said. It was barely audible, an empathetic whisper, like he knew her already. Nobody had said her name like that before. Not even her father, who was kind and gentle, too, if remote.

She resolved not to use the box of tissues provided. 'I won't need them,' she thought. But when he uttered her name, paused and waited for her to speak, she suddenly felt a lump in her throat. 'Here was this man. He wasn't talking about himself, his ambitions, his weekend, his ex-girlfriends, he was interested in me. I had spent my life trying to get to know all these men, trying to understand them, figure out how to make them happy. But I'd never got to know myself.'

Helen spoke about her family, her late father, who worked his way into an early grave, her overbearing mother who did her best to hold it all together because what would the neighbours think and, well, just because.

She told her therapist about being the eldest child who had to set an example for her sister and little brother. On her shoulders the reputation and morals of the family. It was an awesome responsibility. She had to work hard, be a loyal friend and neighbour and God forbid if she ever came home pregnant. She became an asset for her parents but lost herself along the way.

The only way to live a life that would show how grateful and appreciative she was for everything – the car she got for her eighteenth birthday, the wardrobe of Lainey Keogh jumpers when they were deemed extravagant even for those who could afford them, the membership of the swanky health club where she could bring her friends and influence people – was to live a life of impeccable morality. She would be there for other people, acquiesce to their demands, become a conduit for other people's wishes. As she had done with her mother.

When she broke up with Andy, the first man she believed she could see herself marrying, all those images disappeared overnight: the white dress, the swanky wedding, the life they would now never have together. Helen went home to Cork and took to her bed.

When she told her mother, she replied, 'You think *my* heart's not broken?'

Even that, her broken heart, did not fully belong to her. She had to offer that up for the souls in purgatory…along with everything else. Like most love between a parent and a child, her mother's love was not 100 per cent unconditional. There was give and take and an element of payback. Her therapist said, 'Your mother and father would probably always love you, no matter what, but in the way they chose to love you. They loved you but they could also choose to withhold that love.'

It could be withdrawn at any time, without a moment's notice, just like her Foreign Legion of men.

During her year in therapy, Helen did the talking for a change and her therapist listened. And she reached for the Kleenex. On the first day, on many days in between. And on the last. She saw herself for the first time through the eyes of an objective bystander. 'It was a fascinating character study,' she says, 'better than any piece of literature, because this was a work in progress and, for the first time, because this was about me. We spend our lives seeking relationships as a cure for all our ills but when we find them, the problems that hold us back don't go away.'

Marcus told her that the relationships we choose bring out those problems rather than make them go away. When we look into another person's eyes, we see ourselves reflected. If we have problems giving love, which Helen didn't, we will see only the problems. If we give too much, which Helen did, we do not see ourselves in our lovers' eyes. We see only them.

'A relationship,' Helen told her therapist, 'can be the loneliest place in the world.' All her relationships had one thing in common: they were with men from a foreign land who would sooner or later go home.

'If they left me, and they did, I didn't have to take it personally. Of course I took it personally but I told myself that it wasn't me; it was the fact that they were always destined to go home. Of course, they could stay, which they never did, or I could join them, which I don't think I was ready to do. It meant I never had to risk being rejected for myself. It was the next worst thing to dating a married man. I chose men who were beautiful and sexy and unavailable.'

She has since met a man from Tallaght. 'I think he's the one,' she says. 'He's from Tallafornia or, as he says, Pram Springs, which is an equally exotic place for me.'

Epilogue

With a broken – or bruised – heart we can limp on to the next chapter. If we learn something from it, it has served its purpose well. The only thing we owe to ourselves is to take the lessons we have learnt from our previous relationship and apply them to the next one. Have we established a negative pattern of behaviour? Do we need to make different choices?

Catherine made a discriminating choice online but when it came to reality, she slept with someone who wasn't right for her, as her parting shot on the Rogaine bottle showed. She was blindsided by her fantasy. She won't be doing that again.

Those who attended Quiet Wednesday were happy to embrace friendship. I felt like a cuckoo, even with my own MaybeFriends.com profile. They were all thoroughly decent people who got swallowed up by the demands of modern life but through the Internet found a way out of it.

Orla and Dan, the missonary and the superhero, had very specific requirements and the online forum to fulfill those needs. Their family is growing. There are still three people in their relationship: Orla, Dan and God. Which is how they like it.

Emily in her empire-line dresses and Anna, who was once legless and shoeless, have beaten the system, by maintaining a sense of humour. So what if Anna's man shared a wardrobe with his non-existent sister or if Emily couldn't face the competition from her farmer's heifers?

Like the sisters, Paisley and Jane, their friendship sees them through.

Timothy, the thirty-eight-year-old serial monogamist, and Sean, the forty-eight-year-old serial singleton, are not dumb blondes. I called them 'The Men Who Knew Too Much' because their self-awareness and sensitivity are at odds with the popular notion of the neanderthal Irish male. Sean's relationship is going strong. Timothy's is over. It takes a special kind of woman to be with men who are so analytical.

Sheila and Eddie are accidental romantics. Eddie's hand was forced by his late brother's bequest of a ceramic egg. They have since moved out of Sheila's pile in Monkstown to a smaller townhouse, where they live like newlyweds, without the ring, with the promise.

Biddy and Barney stayed together through financial hardship. If any of the aforementioned think they have it bad, Biddy and Barney showed a resilience and lightness of touch that should not be forgotten.

Since this book was completed, Harry passed away. I included him because he wanted to be a part of it. I'm glad I recorded his story. His rendition of 'Sweet Sixteen' may have not been what it was when his Kay was alive but he never felt sorry for himself during his years without his beloved. Their cottage now lies empty but Harry's story lives on in these pages.

Michael, the clubber and party animal, has been through the eye of the storm, the strobe lights of club-land, and he has emerged with a wise head on his broad shoulders. He is on a health kick; he works out and it suits him.

Aran has finished college and gone to Sydney. He still dreams that gay marriage will be possible some day. Jennifer and Ciara, the 'Venn Diaphragms', have opened a second restaurant; their personal and professional relationship is as strong as ever.

Maureen and Angela have yet to have that first fight in their forty years of friendship and go ballroom-dancing every week. Nor have Peig and Betty, the bingo ladies, given up their numbers.

Fred and Celeste's book club has not disbanded; Celeste recently turned forty and the couple is now expecting their first child. They are reading Harper Lee's *To Kill a Mockingbird* for their next book club. Danny and Alex remain best friends who can tell each other anything, without judgement calls. Alex will be Danny's best man when Danny marries Alex's sister.

Richard, the man who loved younger women, took early retirement but that has not dulled his love for the fairer sex.

Matthew is single. His many ex-girlfriends are not. Helen and her man from Tallaght are going strong.

As Michael and Catherine show, it's possible to be contentedly single – of course it is – whether we are searching for love, sex, companionship or all the above. But a life without other people? We are not designed to be alone all the time. You could meet someone in a bar, at a book club, by your grandmother's deathbed or on the Internet. They could tell you their life story or just want to be with you; you could live hopefully ever after or you may never see them again. What was important were these moments you had together.

The real-life characters in this book may not all have found their heart's desire but they dust themselves off and try again. None have given up, even if they're not entirely sure what they're after. They do the best they can. The same is true for an advice columnist. It's not the perfect life that informs, it's the drama-filled, mistake-ridden imperfect one.